THE ASIAN FINANCIAL CRISIS
Causes, Cures, and
Systemic Implications

MORRIS GOLDSTEIN

THE ASIAN FINANCIAL CRISIS
Causes, Cures, and Systemic Implications

INSTITUTE FOR INTERNATIONAL ECONOMICS
Washington, DC
June 1998

Morris Goldstein, *Dennis Weatherstone Senior Fellow*, held several senior staff positions at the International Monetary Fund (1970–94), including Deputy Director of its Research Department (1987–94). He has written extensively on international economic policy and on international capital markets. He is coeditor of *Private Capital Flows to Emerging Markets after the Mexican Crisis* (1996), author of *The Case for an International Banking Standard* (1997), and of *The Exchange Rate System and the IMF: A Modest Agenda* (1995).

INSTITUTE FOR INTERNATIONAL
ECONOMICS
11 Dupont Circle, NW
Washington, DC 20036-1207
(202) 328-9000 FAX: (202) 328-5432

C. Fred Bergsten, *Director*
Christine F. Lowry, *Director of Publications*

Typesetting and printing by Automated Graphic Systems

For reprints/permission to photocopy please contact the APS customer service department at CCC Academic Permissions Service, 27 Congress Street, Salem, MA 01970.

Printed in the United States of America
00 99 98 5 4 3 2

Library of Congress Cataloging-in-Publication Data

Goldstein, Morris, 1944-
 The Asian financial crisis : causes, cures, and systemic implications / Morris Goldstein.
  p.   cm. — (Policy analyses in international economics ; 55)
 Includes bibliographical references.
 ISBN 0-88132-261-X
 1. Stock exchanges—Asia, Southeastern. 2. Foreign exchange—Government policy—Asia, Southeastern. 3. Stock exchanges—Asia. 4. Foreign exchange—Government policy—Asia. 5. Financial crises—Asia. 6. International Monetary Fund. I. Institute for International Economics (U.S.) II. Title. III. Series.
 HG5740.8.A3G65   1998
 332'.095—dc21   98-7607
                                  CIP

The views expressed in this publication are those of the author. This publication is part of the overall program of the Institute, as endorsed by its Board of Directors, but does not necessarily reflect the views of individual members of the Board or the Advisory Committee.

Contents

Preface

Currency and other financial crises, and their implications for the international monetary system, have been central features of research at the Institute for International Economics throughout its existence since 1981. In the 1980s, William Cline conducted several pathbreaking studies on Third World debt. Stephen Marris produced the landmark analysis of the risks of a hard landing for the dollar. The Institute developed a number of reform proposals to reduce the likelihood of future crises, including the foundations for the Baker and Brady plans on Third World debt (by Cline and John Williamson, respectively) and the idea for currency target zones (by C. Fred Bergsten and Williamson) that formed the basis for the G-7's Louvre Agreement on "reference ranges."

In the 1990s, the Institute has addressed similar themes. Publications by Wendy Dobson (*Economic Policy Coordination: Requiem or Prologue?*) and by Bergsten and C. Randall Henning (*Global Economic Leadership and the Group of Seven*) explored how G-7 economic policy coordination could be improved and reinvigorated. Morris Goldstein (*The Exchange Rate System and the IMF: A Modest Agenda*) addressed the appropriate role for the IMF in the evolving exchange rate system. Guillermo Calvo, Goldstein, and Eduard Hochreiter (*Private Capital Flows to Emerging Markets After the Mexican Crisis*) delved into the lessons of the Mexican peso crisis of 1994-95. Goldstein (*The Case for an International Banking Standard*) examined the factors behind the rash of banking crises in the developing world over the past 15 years and proposed a voluntary international banking standard (shortly thereafter adopted as the Basle Core Principles) to reduce the incidence of such crises in the future.

In this study, Dennis Weatherstone Senior Fellow Morris Goldstein explains how the ongoing Asian financial crisis arose and spread, outlines corrective policy measures, and proposes a package of improvements in the international framework for crisis prevention and management. The study updates and expands upon an interim report that Dr. Goldstein made last fall to the Washington policy community based on an extended visit to the region.

While Dr. Goldstein argues that the Asian financial crisis had multiple interrelated origins, and that a broad policy response will be necessary to overcome it, his analysis is notable for the emphasis it places on financial-sector weaknesses in the crisis countries as the most important source of vulnerability and as the key locus of reform efforts. Given the heated debate that is now going on about the design and effectiveness of IMF-led official rescue packages—and in the US Congress over further funding for the IMF—one of his most important conclusions is that, with the exception of the moral hazard argument, the criticisms leveled at the IMF are off the mark. Moral hazard is a serious problem, however, and particular attention should thus be paid to Dr. Goldstein's proposals for reducing that risk by increasing the orderliness and flexibility of private debt rescheduling. He also stresses the importance of strengthening prudential/supervisory standards in emerging economies, and of sweetening the incentives for the early adoption of such standards.

The Institute for International Economics is a private nonprofit institution for the study and discussion of international economic policy. Its purpose is to analyze important issues in that area and to develop and communicate practical new approaches for dealing with them. The Institute is completely nonpartisan.

The Institute is funded largely by philanthropic foundations. Major institutional grants are now being received from The German Marshall Fund of the United States, which created the Institute with a generous commitment of funds in 1981, The Andrew W. Mellon Foundation, and The Starr Foundation. A number of other foundations and private corporations also contribute to the highly diversified financial resources of the Institute. The Rockefeller Brothers Fund has provided generous support for Dr. Goldstein's work. The Washington SyCip Family Foundation has enabled us to expand our coverage of ASEAN countries. About 12 percent of the Institute's resources in our latest fiscal year were provided by contributors outside the United States, including about 6 percent from Japan.

The author of the study, Dr. Morris Goldstein, is the Dennis Weatherstone Senior Fellow at the Institute. Our Board of Directors created this endowed chair in honor of Sir Dennis Weatherstone, who retired as Chairman and Chief Executive Officer of J.P. Morgan & Co. Incorporated at the end of 1994, in recognition of his superb service as a member of the Board, a member of its Executive Committee, and Chairman of its Investment Committee throughout the life of the Institute since 1981. Support for the chair has been provided by the Olayan Foundation, J.P. Morgan & Co. Incorporated, the Stavros S. Niarchos Foundation, and the GE Fund.

The Board of Directors bears overall responsibility for the Institute and gives general guidance and approval to its research program—including identification of topics that are likely to become important to international economic policymakers over the medium run (generally, one to three years), and which thus should be addressed by the Institute. The Director, working closely with the staff and outside Advisory Committee, is responsible for the development of particular projects and makes the final decision to publish an individual study.

The Institute hopes that its studies and other activities will contribute to building a stronger foundation for international economic policy around the world. We invite readers of these publications to let us know how they think we can best accomplish this objective.

C. FRED BERGSTEN
Director
May 1998

Acknowledgments

This book is a revised and expanded version of an Institute for International Economics luncheon talk delivered at the Carlton Hotel in Washington on 2 December 1997. It draws heavily on joint work with John Hawkins of the Reserve Bank of Australia on the origins of the crisis, undertaken when I was a visiting economist at that institution in October 1997. I am indebted to C. Fred Bergsten who read the entire manuscript carefully and, as usual, offered a host of valuable suggestions. I am also grateful to Barry Bosworth, Steve Grenville, Graham Hacche, John Hawkins, George Kaufman, Mohsin Khan, Frederic Mishkin, Michael Mussa, Adam Posen, Carmen Reinhart, Glenn Stevens, and Philip Turner for helpful comments and discussions on an earlier draft and to Mark Giancola for superb research assistance. Here at the institute, Brigitte Coulton, Kara Davis, Helen Kim, David Krzywda, and Christine Lowry did a terrific job of getting the published version ready under a very tight deadline. The views expressed are entirely my own, and I bear sole responsibility for any errors and omissions that remain.

1

Introduction

The turmoil that has rocked Asian foreign-exchange and equity markets since June 1997 and that has spread far afield is the third major currency crisis of the 1990s. Its two predecessors were the crisis in the European Monetary System (EMS) of 1992–93 and the Mexican peso crisis of 1994–95.

At the meeting of heads of state of the Asia Pacific Economic Cooperation (APEC) forum in Vancouver in November 1997, US President Bill Clinton first characterized the Asian crisis as "a few small glitches in the road"—a description that has given way to less rosy scenarios as evidence of the depth and breadth of the crisis has accumulated. As shown in tables 1 and 2, currency and equity markets in emerging Asia recorded huge falls—on the order of 30 to 50 percent—in the second half of 1997 (as measured from the end of June, just before the floating of the Thai baht). Developments during the first four months of 1998 have been mixed: on the positive side, there have been some rebounds in exchange rates in Thailand and South Korea and in equity prices in the Philippines; in the negative column, the downward slide in the Indonesian rupiah has accelerated, and even where currency and equity prices have rebounded, the cumulative decline over the crisis period as a whole remains very large.

Moreover, forecasts of 1998 economic growth in the region—which stood in the 6 to 8 percent neighborhood prior to the crisis—have been sharply marked down since then (see table 3).[1] Thailand, Indonesia, and

---

1. Goldstein and Hawkins (1998) show that these downward revisions of 1998 growth forecasts for the Asian emerging economies represent some of the largest downward revisions (over a 6-month period) of the 1990s.

1

Table 1 Exchange rates, 30 June 1997 to 8 May 1998

	US dollars per 100 local currency 6/30/97	US dollars per 100 local currency 12/31/97	Percentage change 6/30/97-12/31/97	US dollars per 100 local currency 5/8/98	Percentage change 1/1/98-5/8/98	Cumulative percentage change 6/30/97-5/8/98
Thailand	4.05	2.08	−48.7	2.59	24.7	−36.0
Malaysia	39.53	25.70	−35.0	26.25	2.1	−33.6
Indonesia	0.04	0.02	−44.4	0.01	−53.0	−73.8
Philippines	3.79	2.51	−33.9	2.54	1.3	−33.0
Hong Kong	12.90	12.90	0.0	12.90	0.0	0.0
Korea, South	0.11	0.06	−47.7	0.07	21.9	−36.2
Taiwan	3.60	3.06	−14.8	3.10	1.2	−13.8
Singapore	69.93	59.44	−15.0	61.80	4.0	−11.6

Sources: Bloomberg; *Financial Times* (various issues).

Table 2 Stock markets, 30 June 1997 to 8 May 1998

	6/30/97	12/31/97	Percentage change 6/30/97- 12/31/97	5/8/98	Percentage change 1/1/98-5/8/98	Cumulative change 6/30/97- 5/8/98
Thailand	527.3	372.7	−29.3	386.4	3.7	−26.7
Malaysia	1,077.3	594.4	−44.8	580.1	−2.4	−46.2
Indonesia	725.0	401.7[a]	−44.6	434.7	8.2	−40.0
Philippines	2,809.0	1,869.2[b]	−33.5	2,210.0	18.2	−21.3
Hong Kong	15,197.0	10,722.8	−29.4	10,060.4	−6.2	−33.8
Korea, South	745.4	376.3[b]	−49.5	373.0	−0.9	−50.0
Taiwan	9,030.0	8,187.3	−9.3	8,210.8	0.3	−9.1
Singapore	1,988.0	1,529.8	−23.0	1,420.8	−7.1	−28.5

Note: All stock market indices are local indices. The Hang Seng index is used for Hong Kong and the Straits Times for Singapore.

a. As of 12/30/97.
b. As of 12/29/97.

Sources: Bloomberg; Financial Times (various issues).

Table 3 Real GDP growth and growth forecasts, 1996-98 (percentages)

			IMF forecasts			Consensus forecasts		
	1996	1997	1998 (as of May 97)	1998 (as of April 98)	Change in 1998 forecast	1998 (as of June 97)	1998 (as of April 98)	Change in 1998 forecast
Indonesia	8.0	5.0	7.4	-5.0	-12.4	7.6	-6.3	-13.9
Thailand	5.5	-0.4	7.0	-3.1	-10.1	5.9	-4.1	-10.0
Korea, South	7.1	5.5	6.3	-0.8	-7.1	6.1	-1.6	-7.7
Malaysia	8.6	7.8	7.9	2.5	-5.4	8.0	1.1	-6.9
Philippines	5.7	5.1	6.4	2.5	-3.9	6.3	2.2	-4.1
Singapore	6.9	7.8	6.1	3.5	-2.6	7.3	2.7	-4.6
Hong Kong	4.9	5.3	5.0	3.0	-2.0	5.5	3.0	-2.5
China	9.7	8.8	8.8	7.0	-1.8	10.4	7.8	-2.6
Taiwan	5.7	6.9	6.3	5.0	-1.3	6.5	5.9	-0.6

Sources: IMF, World Economic Outlook (various issues); Goldstein and Hawkins (1998); Consensus Economics, Inc., Asia-Pacific Consensus Forecasts (June 1997 and April 1998).

South Korea are now expected to suffer recessions this year, and growth in Malaysia and the Philippines is likely to be only about a third of what was anticipated prior to the crisis. Excluding China, growth in emerging Asia is now expected to be only marginally positive (1 to 2 percent) this year.

Moving outside the region, it becomes more hazardous to link changes in 1998 growth forecasts solely to the effects of the Asian crisis, because other factors have also changed. Nevertheless, it is relevant to note that in April 1998 the International Monetary Fund (IMF) (1998b) revised its 1998 global growth projection to 3.1 percent—down from 4.3 percent in October 1997, and (roughly) two-thirds of that downward revision might be attributed to slower growth in developing Asia. Turning to growth in the largest industrial countries, there is a consensus that Japan has been hardest hit by the Asian crisis, with its impact exacerbating Japan's serious homegrown problems.[2] In the United States, the contractionary impact of the Asian crisis has so far been more subdued, and the IMF's latest (1998b) forecast for 1998 growth is in fact now higher than it was before the crisis.[3]

My aim in this book is threefold: first, to explain how the Asian financial crisis arose and spread; second, to outline the kinds of corrective policy measures and reforms that would help to end the crisis; and third, to suggest a package of improvements in the international framework for crisis prevention and crisis management.

Chapter 2 discusses the three main interrelated origins of the crisis, namely: *financial-sector weaknesses* in Asian emerging economies cum easy global liquidity conditions; mounting concerns about *external-sector problems* in these economies; and *contagion* from Thailand—first to three larger economies of the Association of Southeast Asian Nations (ASEAN-4) (Indonesia, Malaysia, and the Philippines), then to North Asia (South Korea, Taiwan, Hong Kong, and Japan), and finally to other countries (ranging from Brazil to Russia and, more briefly, to equity markets in some major industrial countries).

Chapter 3 turns to proposals for fixing the crisis. Here, I take up restructuring and reform of financial sectors and prudential supervision in the ASEAN-4 economies and South Korea, exchange rate policies in Asia, fiscal and financial-sector policies in Japan, competitive depreciation pressures facing China, and the design and effectiveness of IMF-led official rescue packages.

---

2. IMF forecasts for 1998 growth in Japan have fallen from 2.9 percent in the May 1997 *World Economic Outlook* to zero in the April 1998 edition. The IMF (1998b) argues that while the Asian crisis added to the toll, the faltering of Japan's recovery in 1997 primarily reflected problems of its own making, including the large withdrawal of fiscal stimulus when the recovery was not yet firmly established, the bad loan problem cum more generalized financial-sector weaknesses, and delays in the implementation of structural reforms. Posen (forthcoming 1998) comes to a similar conclusion. Liu et al. (1998) also find that Japan's real GDP is more adversely affected by the Asian crisis than either the United States or Europe but emphasize that the outcome is heavily influenced by how one treats the depreciation of the yen vis-à-vis the US dollar and European currencies over the period and by how one accounts for the real absorbtion effects of exchange rate changes. As argued in chapters 2 and 3, Japan's problems have also been an important element in the origins of the crisis and have made recovery from the regional crisis more difficult.

3. In May 1997, the IMF was projecting 1998 growth in the United States to be 2.2 percent; the April 1998 *World Economic Outlook* envisages US growth of 2.9 percent in 1998.

In chapter 4, I put forward a set of "Halifax II" reforms to strengthen what US Treasury Secretary Robert Rubin (1998) has recently called the "international financial architecture."[4] These proposed reforms are grouped under the following five headings: (1) reducing moral hazard and bringing more order and flexibility to private debt rescheduling; (2) strengthening prudential standards in developing countries and making it more attractive for countries to implement these standards sooner; (3) improving transparency and disclosure in international financial markets; (4) giving IMF surveillance more punch; and (5) shoring up risk management in global financial institutions.

Finally, chapter 5 outlines 10 lessons from the crisis and offers some brief concluding remarks about the future role of the IMF.

---

4. The G-7 Economic Summit in Halifax, Canada in June 1995, following the Mexican peso crisis, paid considerable attention to supervisory and global financial-architecture issues.

2

Origins of the Crisis

Financial crises are seldom generated by one or two isolated factors.[1] The Asian financial crisis is no exception. In what follows, I analyze its multiple origins.

Financial-Sector Weaknesses

Each of the ASEAN-4 economies experienced a *credit boom* in the 1990s, that is, the growth of bank and nonbank credit to the private sector exceeded by a wide margin the already rapid growth of real GDP (see part A of table 4). The credit boom was stoked in part by large net private capital inflows and directed in good measure to *real estate and equities*.[2] As illustrated in part B of table 4, exposure to the property sector accounted for roughly 25 to 40 percent of total bank loans in Thailand, Indonesia, Malaysia, and Singapore and more than that in Hong Kong.[3] Data on

1. Goldstein and Reinhart (forthcoming 1998) show that in most emerging-market banking and currency crises of the past 25 years, a high proportion of warning signals were flashing.

2. Montiel and Reinhart (1997) argue that the sterilization policies followed by the host (capital inflow) countries played an important part in setting the stage for the subsequent crisis; specifically, sterilization operations kept domestic interest rates in the host countries higher than would otherwise have been the case, thereby inducing both larger net inflows and a high share of interest-sensitive short-term flows.

3. In Thailand, Indonesia, and Malaysia, this exposure was compounded by high (80 to 100 percent) loan to collateral ratios. Also, most of banks' exposure to the property market reflects exposure to property developers rather than to homeowners; see Goldstein and Hawkins (1998).

Table 4 Growth and composition of bank lending, 1990-96 and 1998

A. Growth of bank credit to the private sector relative to the growth of GDP

	1990-94	1995	1996
Thailand	10.0	11.1	5.8
Indonesia	10.4	4.4	5.7
Malaysia	3.1	10.5	13.1
Philippines	10.7	27.4	31.5
Hong Kong	8.8	8.9	−6.1
Singapore	0.8	7.8	5.7
Korea, South	2.6	2.2	−0.6
Mexico	25.7	−0.6	−36.0

B. Estimates of the share of bank lending to the property sector

	end-1997
Hong Kong	40-55
Singapore	30-40
Thailand	30-40
Malaysia	30-40
Indonesia	25-30
Korea, South	15-25
Philippines	15-20

Sources: Bank for International Settlements (1997); Eschweiler (1998).

exposure of banks to the equity market are harder to come by, but the rising ratio of stock market credit to GDP in Malaysia and the large-scale holdings of equities by South Korean banks have contributed to the strains in these economies.[4]

This overextension and concentration of credit left the ASEAN-4 economies vulnerable to a shift in credit and cyclical conditions. When that shift came, induced initially by the need to control overheating and later on by an export slowdown and by an effort to defend exchange rates with high interest rates against strong market pressures, it brought with it, inter alia, falling property prices and a rising share of nonperforming

---

4. The highly leveraged state of the Malaysian economy may explain why the authorities have been reluctant to use an aggressive interest rate defense to slow the decline in the ringgit. According to estimates reviewed in Eschweiler (1997a), the impact of a rise in the short-term interest rate on GDP is higher in Malaysia than in the other ASEAN-4 economies. Walsh (*Sydney Morning Herald*, 22 October 1997) documents that in 1997 the ratio of stock market credit to GDP in Malaysia was higher than that in the United States just prior to the Great Depression.

bank loans.[5] Reflecting the significant amount of office space coming on stream, most private analysts conclude that the fall in real property prices in Asian emerging economies has still not fully run its course.[6] Because the credit boom began and ended earlier in Thailand and Indonesia than in Malaysia and the Philippines, the effects were first visible in the former two countries.

While there is considerable variation across the different studies, private-sector estimates of peak and actual nonperforming bank loans point to extreme banking difficulties (that is, shares of nonperforming to total bank loans in the 15 to 35 percent range) in Thailand, South Korea, and Indonesia, and some analysts see Malaysia's banking industry as also in bad shape (see table 5).[7] The same studies suggest that banks in the Philippines have not been as devastated as in the worst-hit group but nevertheless are much more fragile than the strong banking systems of Hong Kong and Singapore.[8]

In Thailand and Indonesia, vulnerability was also heightened because banks and/or their corporate customers—in seeking to minimize their borrowing costs—agreed to shoulder rollover and currency risk; that is, *too much of their foreign borrowing was undertaken at short maturities and/or denominated in foreign currency.*[9] At the time, this was not thought to be such a risky strategy because the Thai baht and the Indonesian rupiah had been stable with respect to the US dollar for many years and because the combination of weak economic activity, a huge stock of bad loans in the banking system, and a public antipathy to bailing out banks seemed to point to the continuation of low interest rates in Japan. Nevertheless, these liquidity and currency mismatches eventually took their toll—in motivating speculative attacks, in magnifying the consequences of subse-

---

5. See Bank for International Settlements (BIS) (1997). BIS (1997) also provides evidence that property-price booms in Asian emerging economies have tended to be more pronounced than those in larger industrial countries—an outcome that it attributes in part to the rapid pace of industrialization and urbanization in Asia that in turn contributes to an extremely strong demand for new buildings.

6. See, for example, Eschweiler (1997a).

7. By "peak" nonperforming loans, I mean estimates of the maximum level of nonperforming loans for the duration of the crisis (usually taken to encompass 1998–99).

8. Banks in the Philippines hold relatively high levels of capital (see Eschweiler 1998).

9. The contention that vulnerability was linked to the composition of external borrowing rather than to the overall external debt burden is supported by cross-country comparisons of the ratios of external debt to GDP and external debt to exports. Specifically, only Indonesia among the five most adversely affected Asian economies has a relatively high debt burden relative to exports—and one that is still lower than those of Argentina and Brazil. Relative to GDP, Thailand and the Philippines have higher debt burdens than their neighbors but not ones outside the range experienced by many developing countries. See Radelet and Sachs (1998) and Goldstein and Hawkins (1998).

Table 5 Estimates of actual and peak nonperforming bank loans in selected Asian emerging economies

Study	Thailand	Korea, South	Indonesia	Malaysia	Philippines	Singapore	Hong Kong
Jardine Flemming (1997)							
PNPL/TL	19.3	na	16.8	15.6	13.4	3.8	na
PNPL/GDP	20.0	na	10.8	22.9	7.2	3.8	na
Ramos (1998), Goldman Sachs							
ANPL/TL	18.0	14.0	9.0	6.0	3.0	2.0	2.0
PNPL/TL	>25.0	>25.0	>25.0	12.0-25.0	10.0-15.0	>8.0	>8.0
PNPL/GDP	40.0	34.0	16.0	17.0	7.0	9.0	13.0
Jen (1998), Morgan Stanley							
ANPL/TL	18.0	14.0	12.5	6.0	na	na	na
Peregrine (1997)							
ANPL/TL	36.0[a]	30.0	15.0	15.0	7.0	4.0	1.0
Eschweiler (1998), JP Morgan							
ANPL/TL	17.5	17.5	11.0	7.5	5.5	3.0	1.8
BIS (1997), official estimate for 1996							
ANPL/TL	7.7[b]	0.8	8.8	3.9	na	na	2.7

na = not available
PNPL = Peak nonperforming loans (1998-99)
ANPL = Actual nonperforming loans (1997 or 1998)
TL = Total loans

a. Includes finance companies.
b. Estimate for 1995.

Table 6   Liquidity and currency mismatches as of June 1997

	Ratio of short-term debt to international reserves	Short-term debt as a percentage of total debt	Ratio of broad money to international reserves
Korea, South	3.0	67	6.2
Indonesia	1.6	24	6.2
Thailand	1.1	46	4.9
Philippines	0.7	19	4.9
Malaysia	0.6	39	4.0
Singapore	na	na	1.0

na = not available

Sources: World Bank (1998); Goldstein and Hawkins (1998); IMF, *International Financial Statistics*.

quent exchange rate changes, and in limiting the authorities' room for maneuver in crisis management.[10]

After the Bank of Thailand drained much of its net international reserves in defense of the baht, the rollover of its large short-term debt obligations became problematic. In Indonesia, the main problem was currency mismatching on the part of corporations.[11] Once the value of the rupiah could no longer be assured, and even more so after the currency was floated, belated efforts by Indonesian corporations to hedge their large short foreign-currency position in the market helped to fuel the rupiah's decline. And, as the rupiah fell, its adverse effect on the debt burden of firms only acted to sap market confidence and to stoke the currency's further decline. In South Korea, too, the rollover of short-term foreign-currency-denominated debt—this time on the part of banks—eventually became the action-forcing event of that crisis.

Table 6 presents several indicators of liquidity/currency mismatch for the Asian emerging economies. Taken as a group, these indicators support the view that South Korea, Indonesia, and Thailand were more "mismatched" than their neighbors in the run-up to the crisis.[12] The contrast

---

10. Calvo and Goldstein (1996) show that similar liquidity and currency mismatches made Mexico more vulnerable than its Latin American neighbors to attack in 1994 . Grenville (1998) emphasizes the differences between the effects of hedged versus unhedged exchange rate changes. Mishkin (1997) makes a persuasive case that heavy reliance on foreign-currency-denominated borrowing not only makes it easier to get into a crisis but also makes it harder to get out of one (because the borrowing country cannot reduce the real value of its liabilities by undertaking a devaluation).

11. Perry and Lederman (1998) and Ito (1998a) show that the ratio of external debt (owed to international banks) to international reserves for the nonbank private sector was much higher in Indonesia in mid-1997 than it was in the other four Asian-crisis economies.

12. See also Perry and Lederman (1998) for other indicators of liquidity and currency mismatch, including the ratio of net foreign assets of the banking system to M2 and the ratio of short-term debt owed to international banks to international reserves. They reach a similar qualitative conclusion on the relatively high vulnerability of South Korea, Thailand,

would be even sharper if *net* rather than gross international reserves were used in such ratios, because Thailand's commitments in the forward exchange market and South Korea's lending of reserves to commercial banks meant that the figures on gross reserves conveyed a misleading impression of the authorities' usable liquid assets.[13]

The buildup of credit booms and liquidity/currency mismatches in the ASEAN-4 countries would not have progressed so far had it not occurred against a backdrop of long-standing weaknesses in banking and financial-sector supervision.[14] As in many other emerging economies, loan classification and provisioning practices were too lax.[15] There was too much "connected lending" (lending to bank directors, managers, and their related businesses), with all the attendant dangers of concentration of credit risk and lack of arms-length credit decisions ("crony capitalism"). There was excessive government ownership of, and/or government involvement in, banks.[16] Banks often became the "quasi-fiscal" agents of governments, providing an oblique mechanism for channeling government assistance (off-budget) to ailing industries. In most of these economies (Hong Kong and Singapore are notable exceptions), bank capital was inadequate relative to the riskiness of banks' operating environment.[17] Based on past behavior, there was a strong expectation that, should banks get into trouble, depositors and creditors would get bailed out, and bank supervisors lacked the mandate to counter strong political pressures for

---

and Indonesia—not only within East Asia but also relative to most emerging economies in Latin America.

13. In this connection, Bhattacharya, Claessens, and Hernandez (1997) estimate that on the eve of the Thai crisis, the ratio of short-term gross external liabilities to net international reserves was on the order of six in Thailand versus less than two in Indonesia and less than one in both Malaysia and the Philippines. Ito (1998a) mentions the lending of South Korean reserves to commercial banks in assessing the adequacy of reserves.

14. See Folkerts-Landau et al. (1995) and Lincoln (1997). Common weaknesses in banking supervision in emerging economies are discussed more extensively in Goldstein (1997a), Goldstein and Turner (1996), and IMF (1998a).

15. A common practice, known in the literature as "evergreening," is to provide a troubled borrower with new loans so that he/she can continue to make payments on the old loan. A good loan classification system would grade a loan according to a forward-looking and comprehensive evaluation of the borrower's creditworthiness—not simply on the payment status of the loan; that is, it would evaluate the loan on the basis of the likelihood that the borrower could meet the next 10 payments, not exclusively on whether the borrower made the last payment. In addition, in several of the crisis countries, loans could be delinquent for 6 to 12 months before they were classified as nonperforming (versus 3 months in the US system). See Goldstein (1997a), Basle Committee on Banking Supervision (1997), and IMF (1998a) for further discussion of good loan classification and provisioning practices.

16. See Williamson and Mahar (1998) for figures on the size of the state-owned banking sector in selected emerging economies.

17. See Goldstein and Turner (1996).

regulatory forbearance.[18] On top of all this, the quality of public disclosure and transparency was poor. For example, the 1997 Bank for International Settlements *Annual Report* contains a missing entry for Thailand's share of nonperforming loans in the banking system for 1996, and estimates of nonperforming loans by outside analysts tended to be on the order of two to three times larger than the last published official figures (see table 5). In South Korea, the discrepancy between official and private estimates of nonperforming loans was even larger still.

But how did banks and their customers in these countries obtain the external financing that helped to support such lending decisions? After all, it takes two to tango. It is well to recall that the 1990s were a period of *bountiful global liquidity conditions*. During that time, over $420 billion in net private capital flows went to Asian developing countries. Private capital flows rebounded quickly after the Mexican crisis: 1996 was a record year for private net flows to emerging economies; moreover, spreads declined, maturities lengthened, and loan covenants weakened.[19] The nearness of a major financial center—namely, Tokyo—with extremely low interest rates also gave rise to a large "carry trade," where funds could be borrowed directly from Japanese institutions or intermediated via US lenders. Moreover, the Bangkok International Banking Facility (BIBF)—created with incentives to promote Bangkok as a regional financial center and intended to raise funds from nonresidents and lend them to other nonresidents ("out-out" transactions)—turned out to be merely a conduit for Thai banks and firms to borrow abroad ("out-in" transactions).

Last but not least, and much like Mexico "before the fall," the ASEAN-4 economies were widely viewed by lenders to be among the most attractive sovereign borrowers among emerging markets.[20] After all, over the past decade they had integrated themselves into the world economy and had recorded unusually rapid rates of economic growth, high saving and investment rates, and disciplined fiscal positions. The latter factor may

---

18. Krugman (1998a) and Dooley (1997) stress implicit and explicit government guarantees as a key factor in motivating large capital inflows into these economies. Calomiris (1997) attributes the greater frequency of banking crises in the past several decades primarily to the expansion of the de facto official safety net. Goldstein (1998b) argues that government guarantees need to be viewed in conjunction with financial liberalization and other factors to explain the greater incidence of banking crises during this period. See also the discussion in chapter 3.

19. One recent study by Cline and Barnes (1997) found that the sharp decline in average spreads on emerging-market Eurobonds between the second quarter of 1995 and the third quarter of 1997 was considerably greater than could be accounted for by improved economic fundamentals in the borrowing countries.

20. South Korea, Malaysia, Thailand, and Indonesia were among the group of 10 developing countries that attracted the largest amounts of net private capital flows during 1990–95; see Goldstein and Hawkins (1998). Grenville (1998) provides a summary of many of the strengths of the ASEAN-4 economies prior to the crisis.

also have given lenders confidence that, should local financial institutions encounter difficulties, the public sector would have the resources to provide assistance.[21] In short, (aside perhaps from their financial sectors), they were seen as among the best students in "Policy Reform 101."

External-Sector Problems

In 1996, Thailand had a current account deficit equal to 8 percent of its GDP. Over the 1990s as a whole, Thailand had a cumulative current account deficit equal to 36 percent of its 1996 GDP.[22] In 6 of the past 15 years, Thailand's current account deficit equaled or exceeded 6 percent of GDP. The other ASEAN-4 economies have also run relatively large current account deficits in the 1990s, albeit not as pronounced as in Thailand.

Until quite recently, these current account imbalances were widely viewed as benign. Indeed, it was frequently concluded that these were "good" deficits in two respects: first, they did not reflect a saving-investment deficit in the public sector; and second, foreign borrowing was being used mainly to increase investment (rather than consumption), thereby building the capacity to service those debts. In both these dimensions, Asian current account deficits were frequently said to be more sustainable than Latin American current account deficits.

In the run-up to the crisis, however, there were at least five counts on which *concerns about current account imbalances* in the ASEAN-4 countries could well have become deeper.

First, the *quality of investment* in these countries was less impressive than the quantity. Even investment ratios of 30 to 40 percent do not look so attractive when corporate governance is very poor, when so much of private investment is directed toward either speculative activities (e.g., real estate) or industries where overcapacity was likely to be a problem over the medium term, and when too much public investment is directed toward either overambitious infrastructure projects or inefficient government monopolies. In this connection, a recent World Bank report (1998) documents that incremental capital-output ratios (the inverse of which is sometimes taken to be a proxy for the productivity of investment) increased sharply in Thailand and South Korea as between 1985–90 and 1990–96.

Second, the behavior of *real effective exchange rates* over the past two years or so pointed to a deterioration in competitiveness in much of emerging Asia. The currencies of the ASEAN-4 economies followed the

---

21. See Claessens and Glaessner (1997).

22. See Bhattacharya, Claessens, and Hernandez (1997).

Table 7 External sector problems

	Real effective exchange rate overvaluation (versus June 1987 to May 1997 average)	Current account balance (percentage of GDP)		Merchandise exports (annual percentage growth)	
	June 1997	1995	1996	1995	1996
Thailand	6.7	−7.9	−7.9	23.1	0.5
Indonesia	4.2	−3.3	−3.3	13.4	9.7
Malaysia	9.3	−10.0	−4.9	20.3	6.5
Philippines	11.9	−4.4	−4.7	28.7	18.7
Hong Kong	22.0	−3.9	−1.3	14.8	4.0
Singapore	13.5	16.8	15.7	13.7	5.3
Korea, South	−7.6	−2.0	−4.9	30.3	3.7
Taiwan	−5.5	2.1	4.0	20.0	3.8

Sources: IMF, International Financial Statistics; IMF, World Economic Outlook; JP Morgan website, 1998; Council for Economic Planning and Development, Republic of China, Taiwan Statistical Data Book, 1997.

US dollar down against the Japanese yen in the first half of the 1990s but then followed the dollar up against the yen thereafter. In the process, they recorded an appreciation of their real (trade-weighted) effective exchange rates relative to trend (where trend is captured by the 1987–97 average). By that measure, at the end of June 1997, the Thai baht stood about 7 percent above its long-term average; the corresponding figures for the Indonesian rupiah, the Malaysian ringgit, and the Philippine peso were 4, 9, and 12 percent, respectively (see table 7).[23] To be sure, long-term averages of actual exchange rates should be regarded as only a rough proxy for equilibrium exchange rates. Nevertheless, such calculations convey the strong impression that the ASEAN-4 countries were not experiencing huge misalignments prior to being attacked. At the same time, given that these real appreciations occurred in the context of large current account imbalances, they were a source of increased vulnerability. Here, it is also worth noting that empirical analyses of early-warning indicators of currency and banking crises in emerging economies find that real exchange rate overvaluation has historically been among the very best performing leading indicators.[24]

---

23. As shown in table 7, the Hong Kong dollar was, by this measure, the most overvalued currency. It should be noted, however, that recent research Dodsworth and Mihaljek (1997) and Hawkins and Yiu (1995) indicates that the equilibrium rate for the Hong Kong dollar may well have been appreciating over the 1983–94 period because of large productivity differentials (along classic productivity-bias lines) between tradable and nontradable goods (where tradables include financial services). This would make the overvaluation smaller than such deviation-from-trend figures suggest.

24. See Kaminsky and Reinhart (1996), Goldstein (1998a), and Goldstein and Reinhart (forthcoming 1998).

Third, *1996* was a year in which many emerging Asian economies experienced a significant *slowdown in merchandise export receipts* (see table 7). In Thailand, merchandise exports were practically flat (0.5 percent increase) in 1996, after rising by 23 percent in 1995. In South Korea, merchandise exports grew by less than 4 percent in 1996—a big change from the 30-percent-plus growth rate of a year earlier. In Malaysia, Indonesia, and the Philippines an export slowdown was likewise in evidence, albeit on a more moderate scale. It was recognized at the time that some of the export slowdown was attributable to temporary factors, including a decline in the growth of world trade and an inventory glut in the global electronics industry.[25] Still, the 1996 slowdown probably raised doubts about whether emerging Asia's export machine was going to remain the dominant force it had been in the past.

A fourth element of concern was the *competition faced by the ASEAN-4 economies from China.* More specifically, some analysts perceived a shift in regional comparative advantage toward China and away from the ASEAN-4 economies.[26] I call it a "perceived" shift because the evidence in favor of this view is less than decisive. For example, Kwan (1997) has noted that the share of Japanese foreign direct investment (FDI) going to China was strongly on the rise between 1992 and 1995–96, whereas the share going to the ASEAN-4 countries was constant. He also notes that analyses of the product composition of exports suggest that ASEAN-4 exports are more "similar" to Chinese exports than are exports of some other Asian economies (South Korea, Taiwan, Singapore)—and this could be seen as disadvantageous to the ASEAN-4 in view of China's relatively low labor costs. On the other hand, Fernald, Edison, and Loungani (1998) have conducted a battery of tests on China's export competition with the rest of developing Asia. They report that there was a strong similarity in export growth between greater China and the rest of developing Asia in the 1994–96 period and conclude that export competition from China is

---

25. According to IMF figures, the volume of world trade grew by 5.6 percent in 1996—down from over 9 percent in 1995. Developments in the global electronics industry are important because of the high weight of electronics in total exports for the Asian emerging economies. Hale (1997) reports that the electronics sector accounts for 57 percent of Singapore's exports, 49 percent of Malaysia's, 40 percent of the Philippines', and 17 percent of Thailand's. In a similar vein, Fernald, Edison, and Loungani (1998) calculate the share of semiconductors and some related capital goods in the exports of Asian economies to the United States. Singapore tops the list at 83 percent; the corresponding figures for other emerging Asian economies are as follows: Malaysia, 61 percent; Taiwan, 57 percent; South Korea, 54 percent; the Philippines, 54 percent; Thailand, 37 percent; greater China, 19 percent; and Indonesia, 10 percent. The BIS (1997) reports that US dollar prices of semiconductors declined by roughly 80 percent in 1996.

26. Thurow (1998), for example, has argued that the swing of the ASEAN-4 economies from trade surplus to deficit is directly traceable to China's decision to concentrate on increasing exports as its engine of economic growth.

unlikely to have been an important factor contributing to the 1997 Asian financial crisis.

Fifth, looking down the road for 1998 and 1999, some observers may well have seen (in 1997) the sustainability of Asian external deficits threatened by *overproduction* in certain industries and by *intense export competition* among countries. Concerns about global overproduction have recently been voiced over a set of industries, including some (memory chips, automobiles, steel, petrochemicals, lumber, base metals, frozen chickens, etc.) that are important for Asian emerging economies.[27] In addition, the heavy historical dependence of these countries on export-led growth may have painted a picture of slowing overall growth prospects. On the importing side, given exchange rate and cyclical developments, the United States may have looked to many like the logical candidate to absorb a healthy share of emerging Asia's exports. But the United States was on its way to a current account deficit in 1997 of almost $170 billion. Would US import-competing industries, organized labor, and US policymakers accept passively an increase in the US external deficit to say, $230–300 billion in 1998, while ASEAN-4 countries, South Korea, and Japan increased significantly their import penetration of the US market?[28] Couldn't there be a protectionist backlash in the United States against much increased imports from Asia?

When you put it together—large current account deficits, deteriorating quality of investment, appreciating real exchange rates, a marked export slowdown in 1996, worries about China "eating the lunch" of the ASEAN-4 and concerns about overproduction, intense export competition, and potential protectionist pressures—it's not hard to see why external sector developments in the run-up to the crisis constituted a second element of vulnerability.

Contagion

Any serious analysis of the Asian currency crisis must also accord a role to contagion of financial disturbances. Past empirical work on contagion has established that contagion is typically greater during periods of turbulence than during more tranquil times, that it operates more on regional than on global lines, and that it usually runs from large countries to smaller ones.[29] On this last count, the Asian currency crisis is unusual, in that it originated in a relatively small country (Thailand) and spread to

27. See, for example, Farrow (1997).

28. Hale (1997) has argued that the US current account deficit in 1998 might well increase to $300 billion.

29. See Calvo and Reinhart (1996).

Table 8 Bilateral trade shares with Thailand, 1996

	Exports to Thailand (as a percentage of total exports)
Korea, South	2.0
Indonesia	1.8
Malaysia	4.1
Philippines	3.8
Singapore	5.7
Taiwan	3.1
Hong Kong	1.0

Sources: IMF, Direction of Trade Statistics Yearbook, 1997; Goldstein and Hawkins (1998).

a wide set of economies, both large (South Korea, Japan, Brazil, Russia) and small.[30]

In addressing the issue of what was driving this contagion, it seems unlikely that the main explanation could be bilateral trade or investment shares with Thailand. Given Thailand's size, these bilateral relationships are simply too small to generate such wide-ranging contagion (see table 8). In addition, if it were bilateral linkages with Thailand that were paramount for the pattern of contagion, one would have expected to see Malaysia, Singapore, and Taiwan more affected than either Indonesia or South Korea—the opposite of what has in fact taken place.[31]

There are, instead, two more-plausible channels of contagion. One is the "wake-up call" hypothesis. In short, it says that Thailand acted as a wake-up call for international investors to reassess creditworthiness of Asian borrowers, and when they did that reassessment, they found that quite a few Asian economies had weaknesses similar to those in Thailand, namely: weak financial sectors with poor prudential supervision, large external deficits, appreciating real exchange rates, declining quality of investment, export slowdowns (in 1996), and overexpansion in certain key industries. As countries were written down to reflect this reassessment of creditworthiness, the crisis spread. Goldstein and Hawkins (1998) show that a weighted average of fundamentals that gives higher weight to those fundamentals where Thailand was relatively weak is more consistent with the ordinal ranking of which Asian economies were most affected by the crisis than are rankings predicated on either the extent of bilateral

---

30. In the case of Japan, however, it would be more accurate to say that lines of causation ran in both directions.

31. See Goldstein and Hawkins (1998).

interdependence with Thailand or the strength of fundamentals irrespective of similarities with Thailand.[32]

I refer to it as a wake-up call because to judge from most market indicators of risk, private creditors and rating agencies were asleep prior to the outbreak of the Thai crisis.[33] Eschweiler (1997a) shows that offshore interest rate spreads on three-month government securities gave no warning of impending difficulties for Indonesia, Malaysia, and the Philippines and produced only intermittent signals for Thailand.[34] Sovereign credit ratings issued by the major private credit-rating agencies were even less prescient. As documented in several studies (Radelet and Sachs 1998; World Bank 1998), long-term sovereign ratings issued by Moody's and Standard and Poors remained unchanged during the 18 month run-up to the crisis.[35]

The second channel of contagion results from the *competitive dynamics of devaluation*. As one country after another in a region undergoes a depreciation of its currency, the countries that have *not* devalued experience a deterioration in competitiveness, which in turn makes their currencies more susceptible to speculative attacks. In short, what was an equilibrium exchange rate *before* competitor countries devalue is not likely to remain

---

32. Goldstein and Hawkins (1998) measure the relative impact of the crisis on individual Asian emerging economies by the decline in exchange rates and equity prices in the second half of 1997 and by the revision in forecasted 1998 real GDP growth rates between June and December 1997. Their measures of bilateral interdependence with Thailand include export shares, geographic distance, telephone traffic with Thailand, and export similarity to Thailand. The fundamentals they consider include: excess credit growth, the ratio of short-term external debt to international reserves, the ratio of broad money to reserves, the ratio of external debt to GDP, the banking system's risk-weighted capital ratio, a median estimate of the share of nonperforming bank loans, Moody's financial-strength bank credit ratings, the ratio of the current account deficit to GDP, international reserves, the extent of the 1996 export slowdown, and three alternative measures of overvaluation of the real exchange rate. Further details of this calculation are available from the authors upon request.

33. Two alternative explanations for why market signals did not produce much early warning of the crisis are that creditors did not have accurate information on the creditworthiness of Asian borrowers (e.g., external debt turned out to be much larger, and international reserves much smaller, than indicated by publicly available data) and that creditors were awake but expected governments (and/or the IMF) to bail them out in case of trouble.

34. As regards exchange market pressures, Eschweiler (1997b) notes that there was some indication of concerns in the unregulated options market for Thai baht (in addition to some earlier attacks on the baht) but also that the Indonesian rupiah was trading on the strong side of its intervention band right up to the outbreak of the crisis. Equity prices turned in a more mixed performance (Eschweiler 1997b; Radelet and Sachs 1998). The Thai, Malaysian, Filipino, and South Korean stock markets were in decline prior to the crisis, but in South Korea's case, the decline began so early that its interpretation is ambiguous; also, equity prices were not declining in the case of Indonesia.

35. The sovereign ratings issued by Euromoney and Institutional Investor did not perform well either. Much the same could be said for stand-alone credit ratings for individual Thai banks.

Table 9 Asian intraregional trade, 1996

| | Export share (as a percentage of total exports) | |
	Emerging Asia	Japan
Thailand	36.8	16.8
Korea, South	37.8	12.3
Indonesia	26.4	28.8
Malaysia	46.8	13.4
Philippines	25.7	17.9
Hong Kong	47.2	6.6
China	37.3	20.4

Source: Lipsky, Brainard, and Parker (1997).

an equilibrium rate *after* the fact. These competitive dynamics of successive devaluations were a factor in the ERM crisis of 1992–93, and they provide a partial explanation for why some Asian currencies came under increasing pressure after the initial depreciations of the Thai baht and Indonesian rupiah. As shown in table 9, the Asian emerging economies have important trade links with one another, and they also compete in third-country markets. Indeed, it is because of these competitive pressures that Williamson (1996) has proposed that these countries adopt a common currency peg. The mechanism of competitive devaluation also explains why questions continue to be asked about whether China will eventually be pressured to devalue (so as to offset the decline in competitiveness linked to the depreciations of the Asian-crisis countries).

Some even go farther (with this competitive devaluation story) and regard the 1994 currency reform cum devaluation of the Chinese yuan as initiating the 1997 round of devaluations. I find this claim unpersuasive. Because of the large share of transactions conducted in the parallel exchange market before the 1994 reform (probably as high as 80 percent), the "effective" devaluation itself was not so large;[36] in addition, China has run higher inflation rates than the (trade-weighted) average of its main trading partners in the 1990s. The bottom line is that China experienced a significant real *appreciation* of its effective exchange rate from the first quarter of 1994 through 1997 (on the order of 50 percent).[37] To the extent that there is evidence of intense export competition between China and the rest of emerging Asia, it takes place in 1989–93—not since then.[38]

---

36. See Liu et al. (1998) and Fernald, Edison, and Loungani (1998). According to Fernald, Edison, and Loungani (1998), the effective nominal depreciation relative to the US dollar was roughly 7 percent.

37. See Fernald, Edison, and Loungani (1998).

38. See Fernald, Edison, and Loungani (1998).

The *contagion to South Korea* is not hard to understand.[39] As noted earlier, South Korea—like Thailand—was an outlier as regards liquidity/maturity mismatches. In addition, it shared with the other Asian-crisis countries long-standing and serious weaknesses in its financial sector and in prudential oversight of banks—much of it tied to government-directed lending to large corporations (*chaebols*), large equity holdings by banks, lax accounting procedures, and a lack of transparency on the part of both banks and corporations. Moreover, the *chaebols* have very high debt-to-equity ratios, and 1996 saw about half of the most important *chaebols* either declare bankruptcy or post losses. By mid-1997, the equity market had already fallen by 60 percent from its previous peak.

Nor can the contagion to *Japan* be considered a matter of financial disturbances elsewhere in the region spilling over to an otherwise healthy economy. Japan has been delinquent in not dealing forcefully and directly with the now-long-standing and massive bad loan problem in its financial sector (recently acknowledged by Japanese authorities to be roughly 80 trillion yen in the banking system). Economic growth in the 1990s has been slower there (on average) than anywhere else in the G-7, and recent projections—including a recent (April 1998) IMF (1998b) forecast of zero growth in 1998—suggest that recovery (along with a rebound in property prices) is still some way off. The long-running steep decline in the equity market has also meant that Japanese banks, which count unrealized gains in their equity holdings as part of their capital, have on several occasions come under risk of breaching their regulatory capital requirements, with consequences not only for their funding costs in the interbank market (the so-called "Japan premium") but also for concerns about forced asset sales to a declining market.[40]

Against this background, it is not surprising that the crisis in emerging Asia—with its adverse implications for Japanese exports and bank loans to these countries and with its spillover to the Japanese equity market—has taken a toll on Japan. As indicated in table 10 Japan conducts a larger share of its total trade with the Asian-crisis countries than does any other G-7 country.[41] Similarly, the World Bank (1998) has estimated that loans to the Asian-crisis countries account for 43 percent of the capital of Japanese banks (versus 27 percent for the G-7 countries as a group).

---

39. Young and Kwon (1998) provide an in-depth analysis of South Korea's vulnerabilities prior to the crisis.

40. For further discussion and explanation for Japan's poor economic performance in the 1990s, see Posen (forthcoming 1998).

41. The geographic pattern of Japanese foreign trade exaggerates the impact of the crisis on Japanese GDP (at least relative to the European G-7 countries) because Japan has much lower ratios of trade to GDP than do the European G-7 countries; see IMF (1997b). In addition, the impact of the crisis on Japan depends, as noted earlier, on whether one includes (as part of the crisis) the depreciation of the yen against the US dollar and European currencies over this period (see Liu et al. 1998).

Table 10 Industrial countries' merchandise trade shares with Asian economies (as a percentage of total trade)

	ASEAN-4 countries	Asian newly industrialized economies	Asian newly industrialized and developing economies	Major emerging market economies
United States	5.0	11.3	21.8	36.7
Japan	12.2	18.2	40.9	43.7
Germany	2.0	3.5	8.6	17.9
France	1.5	2.8	7.4	10.3
Italy	1.4	2.9	6.7	15.0
United Kingdom	2.5	5.2	10.3	14.7
Canada	1.2	2.8	5.9	8.6
G-7 total	4.3	7.9	17.0	24.9

Source: IMF, *World Economic Outlook: Interim Assessment, December 1997.*

And as the number of countries affected by the crisis has grown, the normal channels of trade and capital flow interdependence have also been at work, including some linkages that help to explain the contagion to emerging economies outside the region. For one thing, the crisis-induced growth slowdown in Asia has contributed to a *weakening of primary commodity prices* that puts downward pressure on economies that depend heavily on such goods for exports.[42] For example, Mexico, Venezuela, and Ecuador have been adversely affected by the decline in oil prices. Because more of its total exports go to Asia than do the exports of any other Latin American economy and because copper bulks large in its exports, Chile has also been relatively hard hit by the feedback from the Asian crisis. Less expected, difficulties at South Korean banks have had knock-on effects as far away as Russia and Brazil, because these banks were heavy purchasers of Russian GKOs (government bonds) and Brazilian Brady bonds and because they liquidated much of their holdings during the turmoil. And on and on.[43]

---

42. See Perry and Lederman (1998).

43. The emphasis in this chapter has been on the underlying vulnerabilities and transmission mechanisms that were responsible for the Asian financial crisis. A different question is whether it is possible to identify clear, short-run triggers for the crisis—much in the same way that the negative outcome of the Danish referendum on the European Monetary Union was a key event for the 1992 ERM crisis or that the Colosio assassination of March 1994 was a key event in the run-up to the Mexican peso crisis. While a host of candidates have been proposed as triggers for the first or second wave of attacks—ranging from heightened expectations of yen appreciation and/or of interest rate increases in Japan in the late spring of 1994, to the devaluation of the new Taiwan dollar in October 1997, to alleged IMF-generated panic associated with its structural policy recommendations for Thailand and Indonesia, and to negative terms-of-trade shocks for key Asian export goods in 1996 and 1997—I confess to finding each of these factors less convincing as triggers than some key events in the two earlier major exchange rate crises of the 1990s.

3

How to Fix It

Just as the crisis did not arise from a single source, there is not a single silver bullet that will fix it. The main policy imperatives are summarized below.

Restructuring and Reform of Financial Sectors and Prudential Oversight in the ASEAN-4 Economies and South Korea

Because it was neglect of financial-sector reform that—more than anything else—got these countries into trouble, such reform has to be the centerpiece of the recovery package.

Each of these countries—with the assistance of the IMF and the World Bank—needs to evaluate to what extent its financial sector was subject to excess capacity prior to the crisis. The larger was this excess capacity, the stronger the case for encouraging the exit of firms as part of restructuring the financial sector. Banks and finance companies that are clearly insolvent should be closed down, while those that are undercapitalized should be recapitalized to meet international capital standards.

Foreign-ownership limits should be liberalized so that foreign financial-service companies can help to finance this recapitalization and contribute to better risk diversification and a strengthening of overall credit and risk management systems. A recent World Bank study by Claessens (1998) demonstrates that the emerging-market banking systems that exhibit relatively high levels of foreign participation (as measured by the ratio of the number of foreign banks to total banks) are also the ones that show lower intermediation costs (as measured by the ratio of overhead costs to total assets) and lower levels of banking fragility (as measured by a Goldman-Sachs index of fragility). Stronger domestic firms should also be encouraged to take over weaker ones, so long as such mergers do not conflict with the need to eliminate overcapacity in the system.

Small retail depositors of failed banks should be paid off. As a quid pro quo for injection of public funds, equity holders of failed banks/ finance companies should lose their stakes and the management of these failed institutions should be fired (and prosecuted, if found to have engaged in fraudulent practices). Large uninsured creditors of closed institutions (both domestic and foreign) should be placed at the back of the queue and should be paid off only to the extent that there is anything left over after the sale of the closed institutions' assets is used to reimburse the deposit insurance fund or treasury (more on this later on in this chapter).

Each of these countries, likewise, needs to commit itself to *upgrading significantly its system of financial-sector supervision and regulation*. The emphasis here should be on making loan classification and provisioning practices stricter, adopting international accounting standards, privatizing state-owned banks and curtailing policy-directed lending, putting tighter controls on connecting lending, and instituting better monitoring and control of banks' foreign-exchange exposure (including large currency mismatching by banks' customers).[1] The most efficient way to encourage this upgrading of prudential standards is to ask these countries to sign on to the Basle Committee on Banking Supervision's "Core Principles of Effective Banking Supervision" (the Core Principles) and to assign the IMF and the World Bank the task of monitoring their compliance with these principles. The Core Principles are reproduced in the appendix.

Table 11 lists the major financial restructuring elements that are included in the IMF-led rescue packages for Thailand, Indonesia, and South Korea. At this point, the restructuring and reform process is still in a relatively early stage in each of the most adversely affected crisis countries. That being said, the design of the reform measures is clearly in the right direction, in the sense that some insolvent institutions are being closed, capital requirements are being increased, foreign-ownership limits and restrictions are being eased, and supervisory practices are being adjusted upward toward international standards. Bright spots over the past three to four months include the decision of the Thai authorities to close (and keep closed) 56 (out of 58) insolvent finance companies, the recent decision (early April 1998) by the Indonesian authorities to close

---

1. I have laid out the elements of what should be included in a minimum set of international banking standards in Goldstein (1997a).

Table 11 Financial restructuring measures agreed upon with IMF

Thailand Measures	Dates	South Korea Measures	Dates	Indonesia Measures	Dates
Suspension of 58 insolvent finance companies.	8/97	New legislation governing supervision, deposit insurance, closure of financial institutions, and allocation of losses and equity write-downs.	12/97	Closure of 16 insolvent banks; conditional liquidity support to others.	11/97
Tightened loan classification and bank licensing rules.	11/97	Closure of 10 (of 14 suspended) merchant banks.	1/98	Placement of weak regional development banks under BI supervision.	12/97
Guidelines for assessment of owners, board members, and managers of financial institutions.	12/97	Submission of rehabilitation plans by remaining merchant banks; recapitalization plans required of commercial banks whose 1997 capital adequacy ratios fall below 8 percent based on full provisioning.	2/98	Establishment of Indonesia Bank Restructuring Agency (IBRA); external guarantees to all creditors and depositors of all locally incorporated banks; compensation of small depositors of closed banks.	1/98
Amendment of bankruptcy laws; stronger loan classification and provisioning rules to meet international standards by 2000.	3/98	Establishment of units at Ministry of Finance and Economy and under Financial Supervisory Board to coordinate and monitor bank restructuring and provision of public funds.	3-4/98	Transfer of 54 weak banks to IBRA; new loan classification and provisioning rules based on international standards.	2/98
Preparation of restructuring and privatization plan for intervened banks; review of banking supervision laws.	6/98	Initiation of consultations with banking community and outside experts on strengthening prudential regulations (regulations to be issued 8-11/98).	4/98	Merger of two state-owned banks; legislation enabling state bank privatization and removing limits on private ownership of banks; establishment of new asset resolution entity.	6/98
Memoranda of understanding with financial institutions on implementing stricter loan classification and provisioning rules.	8-9/98	Legislation to allow full write-down of existing share-holders' equity.	6/98	Portfolio, systems, and financial review of IBRA and major non-IBRA banks by internationally recognized audit firms.	8/98
Revision of Bank of Thailand laws; completion of amendments to foreclosure laws.	10/98			Preparation of restructuring plan for IBRA banks	10/98
Completion of disposal of assets of 56 (of 58 suspended) finance companies; new prudential regulations; stronger rules governing disclosure, auditing, and accounting practices; new deposit insurance scheme.	12/98			Preparation of state banks for privatization.	2001
Development of plans for privatizing institutions undergoing state intervention.	nd			Introduction of deposit-insurance scheme.	nd

Sources: Thailand's Letters of Intent to the IMF (25 November 1997 and 24 February 1998); Indonesia's Letters of Intent to the IMF (15 January 1998 and 10 April 1998); South Korea's Letters of Intent to the IMF (3 December 1997, 24 December 1997, and 7 February 1998).

nd = no date specified.

25

14 more weak banks (they had closed 16 banks in November 1997), and South Korea's commitment to upgrade its prudential and supervisory structure by signing on to the Core Principles. What remains to be seen is whether the restructuring and reform process will be sustained over the next two to three years, particularly as it faces resistance from industrial and family groups who will lose favored access to cheap credit, as consolidation forces layoffs in the industry against a backdrop of recession and slow growth in the economy more generally, and as foreign banks gain market share in the industry.

Exchange Rate Policies in Asia and Trade Policies in the G-7

For the foreseeable future, the *crisis countries should not attempt a return to fixed exchange rates*. Instead, they should stick with a managed float. Defense of a fixed exchange rate requires active use of interest-rate policy to squeeze short sellers during speculative attacks. But high interest rates—other than for a short period—will not be credible in countries where weak financial sectors are in the process of being restructured and where growth rates are well below precrisis levels; in these conditions, the costs of "holding on" (to the peg) become too large relative to the (credibility) costs of reneging. Markets realize this. This is likely to be the situation for two or three years—not two or three months. In this connection, Goldstein and Reinhart (forthcoming 1998) report that judging from earlier banking crises in emerging economies over the past 25 years, it takes about 2 to 3 years before growth rates in crisis countries return to the average of the two precrisis years. Hong Kong and Argentina have thus far fared better in the crisis than some of their neighbors *not* because they have currency boards but rather because they have gone farther in strengthening their banks and their liquidity defenses; so too with Singapore (which has a more flexible exchange rate regime).

This change in (emerging Asia's) exchange rate regimes toward much greater flexibility will, however, bring with it certain threats that were not so pressing prior to the crisis. By now, there is wide-ranging evidence that volatility of real exchange rates is typically higher under floating than under fixed exchange rate regimes.[2] Also, weak domestic demand and high shares of exports in GDP (see table 12) will put a lot of pressure on crisis countries to export their way out of recession. Given the size of devaluations in Asian crisis countries, one should expect import penetration to rise sharply in some of the industrial countries contributing to the rescue packages—especially the United States, where, as noted earlier,

---

2. See Mussa (1986) for a summary of that evidence.

Table 12   Asian export to GDP ratios, 1996

	Exports as a percentage of GDP
Thailand	30.2
Korea, South	26.8
Indonesia	21.9
Malaysia	78.8
Philippines	24.4
China	21.2[a]
Hong Kong	117.3
Taiwan	42.5
Singapore	132.9

a. 1995.

Source: IMF, International Financial Statistics.

the 1997 current account deficit of roughly $170 billion is headed sharply upward this year. Thus far, the turnaround in the current account position of the Asian-crisis countries has come much more from a reduction in imports than from an expansion of exports (perhaps reflecting credit and debt-servicing difficulties on the part of exporters in the crisis countries), but the export expansion should gain momentum in the second half of 1998.[3] Press reports suggest that some import-competing industries in the major industrial countries (e.g., Dynamic Random Access Memory [DRAM] producers) are already gearing up for antidumping complaints (*New York Times*, 1997).

In view of all this, it would not be surprising if charges of *competitive depreciation* and exchange rate manipulation begin to surface (both within emerging Asia and in the United States and the European Union). It is well to recall that such charges were a temporary feature of the post-ERM crisis landscape—the core countries (especially France and Germany) complained about the "excessive" depreciation of the lira, the pound, the Swedish kroner, the Spanish peseta, and the Portuguese escudo. Already, in this crisis charges have been made that Taiwan did not defend its currency forcefully enough in October 1997 and that its devaluation added unduly to the pressure on Hong Kong.[4] The fact that no consensus presently exists over what kind of behavior constitutes competitive depreciation or exchange rate manipulation under today's international monetary system only adds to the problem.

---

3. See Goldstein and Hawkins (1998).

4. See Bergsten (1997, 3) who concludes that Taiwan's action represented "a clear competitive devaluation reminiscent of the 1930s."

This means that Asian countries along with the G-7 will need to *consult and cooperate more closely on exchange rate policies* than they have in the past. As recovery from the crisis takes hold and as domestic demand and exchange rates in the crisis countries strengthen, this threat will become less acute—but it will be important in the interim. This is an area where regional cooperation groups (APEC, Executive Meeting for East Asia Pacific [EMEAP], etc.), along with the IMF, can be helpful in defusing incipient tensions and providing a dialogue on exchange rates and supporting policies.

On the trade policy side, the major industrial countries likewise need to resist actions that would frustrate or handicap the adjustment underway in the Asian-crisis countries. In particular, as suggested by Bergsten (1998), the *major industrial countries should not adopt any new trade restrictions in the wake of the Asian crisis.*

Japan's Role

Japan has to become part of the solution to the crisis—not a tinder box that handicaps crisis management. For that to happen, domestic demand in Japan has to resume satisfactory rates of growth, and Japan has to get its bad-loan problem behind it.

As the economic situation in Japan has continued to deteriorate over the past few months, a crescendo has been building for bold fiscal expansion. With interest rates (at both the short and long ends of the yield curve) at historic lows, with the standard cyclical indicators pointing in a recessionary direction, with aggregate price indices signaling zero inflation or deflation, with recent fiscal policy actually withdrawing stimulus from the economy, with a structural (cyclically adjusted) budget deficit less than half as large as the actual one and an extremely low ratio of net government debt to GDP, and with recession working strongly against a recovery of property prices and a decline in bankruptcies (both of which exacerbate the bad loan problem), it's hard to imagine a conjuncture more favorable to strong fiscal policy stimulus.

The chorus of external and internal calls for bolder fiscal action elicited in March 1998 announcements from the Japanese authorities that they are prepared to go forward with a 16 trillion yen fiscal package. A useful assessment of this proposal—which I support—is contained in a forthcoming IIE study by Posen (forthcoming 1998). He notes that over the past decade the net stimulus associated with announced Japanese fiscal packages has typically been much smaller than meets the eye because, inter alia, previously planned expenditures are often simply moved forward from the next year's budget and because asset purchases and transfers (which often loom large in these packages) have very small aggregate demand effects. If this package falls on the regression line, the 16 trillion yen would really be half as large in *net* terms. Posen (forthcoming 1998) argues that, given Japan's present output gap of about 3 percent, a net stimulus package of 16 trillion yen would be about the right size. When fiscal stimulus has been significant (as in 1995), it did have significant output effects (as in 1996).[5] Furthermore, Posen concludes that most of the stimulus should take the form of personal tax cuts rather than further increases in public spending because: (1) consumption in Japan is particularly weak, whereas there is overinvestment and low efficiency in the areas typically targeted for public investment; (2) cuts in tax revenue will induce falls in public expenditure in the medium term (thus helping to deal with Japan's longer-term fiscal problem); (3) overall resource allocation will be improved by moving resources from the public to the private sector; and (4) the difference in the multipliers as between expenditure increases and tax cuts is considerably smaller in the long run than in the short run.[6] To sum up, a 16 trillion yen fiscal stimulus would be a big improvement over the previously announced 2 trillion yen package; it would be even better if it were really a 16 trillion yen addition to the status quo (rather than some fraction of it) and if permanent tax cuts (rather than expenditure increases) were the focal point of the package.

The good news on the bad loan problem is that the authorities have finally discarded the fantasy that they will be able to overcome widespread banking fragility without a sizeable injection of public funds and have indicated that they will increase their initial proposal of a 10 trillion yen injection to 30 trillion yen. The bad news is that much of this money may go to propping up insolvent or very weak banks, that earlier announced plans to implement rules-based "prompt corrective action" procedures may well be postponed, and that various "gimmicks" may be employed to artificially inflate regulatory bank capital and to offset the (welcome) move to more rigorous loan classification procedures.[7] The risks here are that the problem of overcapacity in the banking industry will remain, that banking supervisors will continue to grant forbearance to undercapitalized banks (rather than compel them to implement corrective actions), and that accounting gimmicks will convey the impression that little has

---

5. Ito (1998b) comes to a similar conclusion, arguing that if the Japanese government had not implemented the fiscal packages of the past five years, real output growth, instead of being merely marginally positive, would actually have been negative.

6. Ito (1998b) also argues that a tax cut is preferable to increased expenditure on public works (because fiscal spending has been wasteful from the supply-side point of view and because a tax cut would boost consumer confidence). He argues further for temporary consumption tax reduction in housing-related expenditures because efforts to increase housing size would have positive feedback effects on consumption.

7. One such accounting gimmick is to allow banks to use the higher of book value or market value in valuing gains or losses on their equity holdings.

changed on transparency and disclosure—with predictable effects on market confidence.

The greatest contribution Japan can make to ending the Asian financial crisis is get its own house in order. It should do so with a sense of urgency. A domestic-demand-led recovery in Japan would allow it to absorb its fair share of exports from emerging Asia and would (cum higher Japanese interest rates) help to end the downward slide of the yen (which, in turn, exacerbates the situation of the Asian-crisis countries, makes it harder for China to resist a devaluation, and threatens to stoke later protectionist pressures in the United States). A significant reduction in the overhang of bad loans would not only feed back positively on Japan's own performance (by easing the credit crunch and building confidence) but would also increase the room for maneuver in rescheduling the bad loans of banks in the crisis countries. At present, regional crisis management is severely handicapped by the constraint that any measures that add (directly or indirectly) to the already serious problems of Japan's banks tend to be avoided—even if such measures would otherwise be helpful in dealing with the crisis.

China's Role

China can play its part in the broader crisis-management strategy by continuing to resist the temptation to devalue its own currency, at least until recovery from the crisis is more firmly established.[8] This should not require a large sacrifice on China's part. China is not under strong immediate pressure to devalue. It has a sizeable stock of international reserves, has been running a small current account surplus, and has a very low ratio of external debt to GDP and to international reserves.[9] Moreover, the low share of portfolio flows in its total capital inflows, the lack of capital account convertibility, and the absence of a deliverable forward market for the currency suggest that there isn't an obvious "foreign fuse" to ignite a speculative attack.[10] Also, given the likely negative effect that an immediate Chinese devaluation would have on confidence and exchange rates in the Asian-crisis countries (including the ability of the Hong Kong authorities to maintain their peg), the net effect of Chinese devaluation on its competitiveness is uncertain

---

8. Bergsten (1998) has characterized China's behavior in the Asian financial crisis thus far as exemplary.

9. China holds approximately $145 billion of international reserves; it ran current account surpluses equal to about 1 and 2.5 percent of GDP in 1996 and 1997, respectively; and its ratio of external debt to GDP is below 20 percent. Perry and Lederman (1998) show that China's ratio of external debt (owed to international banks) to international reserves in mid-1997 was much below that in the Asian-crisis countries.

10. See Lardy (1998).

but likely to be considerably smaller than the gross effect. Indeed, because of its spillover effects within the region, an early Chinese devaluation might even worsen China's competitive position. In any case, China has not yet suffered a large deterioration in competitiveness because of the devaluations in the Asian-crisis countries. Liu et al. (1998) have estimated that roughly a 6 percent real devaluation of the renminbi would be sufficient to offset the balance of payments effects of the devaluations that have occurred in Asia since the crisis began—that is, to restore the status quo ante.

But what is true in the short term is not necessarily so beyond that.[11] China is facing a serious problem in downsizing and reforming its loss-making state-owned enterprises. These losses have increasingly been financed not through the budget but rather by relying on loans from the state-owned banks. As a result, China's state-owned banks are now burdened with a share of nonperforming loans that matches or exceeds the worst cases among the Asian-crisis countries.[12] As Lardy (1998) argues convincingly, failure to deal promptly and forcefully with this banking problem would seriously handicap reform efforts in other areas (ranging from establishing capital account convertibility to developing China's bond and equity markets), would lower saving and hinder the efficient allocation of investment, and would run the risk of igniting a domestic bank run. But restructuring state-owned enterprises and recapitalizing the state owned banks is likely to be expensive—both in terms of short-term employment losses and fiscal costs. As Fernald, Edison, and Loungani (1998) show, the Asian financial crisis has already increased the risk premium on Chinese sovereign debt and is likely to slow FDI flows into China. All of this is occurring against a backdrop of an already severe urban unemployment problem (with all its social repercussions) and a projected slowing of GDP growth for 1998.[13] It would not be surprising therefore if China saw a no devaluation pledge as too costly beyond the next two years or so.

IMF Rescue Packages

Turning to the *design and effectiveness of IMF-led rescue packages, much of the criticism that has surfaced in recent months is off the mark.* Indeed, of the five most frequently voiced criticisms, three stand on very weak ground,

---

11. This issue is discussed more fully in Lardy (1998), Liu et al. (1998), and Fernald, Edison, and Loungani (1998).

12. See Lardy (1998) and Liu et al. (1998).

13. The April 1998 IMF *World Economic Outlook* projects that China's real GDP growth will slow from 8.8 percent last year to about 7 percent this year.

and one is a toss-up. The only criticism that really hits home is the moral hazard problem linked to bailing out large uninsured creditors of banks in the crisis countries (primarily in South Korea).

One critique says that the strong medicine prescribed by the IMF for the crisis countries is ill advised because these countries were well behaved before the crisis. They were merely "victims" of a marked and concerted shift in the sentiment of investors cum contagion.[14] This argument ignores the serious financial-sector weaknesses and external-imbalance problems (outlined above) in the crisis countries. In short, banks and corporations let short-term and foreign-currency borrowing get out of hand to finance expansion, and they used the proceeds unwisely—this eventually came back to bite them. This interpretation does not preclude overshooting by the market once the crisis got started, but it rejects the "innocent bystander" hypothesis. The fact that the market did not see the crisis coming likewise does not indicate that fundamentals were fine. Empirical work by Goldstein and Reinhart (forthcoming 1998) on more than 120 banking and currency crises in emerging markets over the past 25 years reveals that interest rate spreads and credit ratings have typically been relatively poor predictors of these crises. In that sense, the Asian financial crisis is hardly unique.

A second line of criticism is that (with the evolution of the international monetary system to floating exchange rates) the IMF is really no longer needed to deal with such crises and that its intervention only serves to delay adjustment.[15] This confuses the exchange rate regime with the IMF's key purpose, namely, providing conditional financing so that countries can deal with balance of payments problems in a way that is less destructive of international prosperity. Without access to such financing, countries would respond to external deficits with larger deflations and greater resort to competitive depreciations and trade and exchange controls (as dramatically illustrated by the experience of the 1920s and 1930s). Even with a near $50 billion rescue package, Mexico underwent a 6 percent decline in real output in 1995—its deepest recession in 50 years. Prior to the crisis, 1998 growth in Thailand was projected to be 7 percent; it is now expected (even with the $17 billion rescue package) to come in between minus 3 and 4 percent. As documented in chapter 1, projected growth rates in the other crisis countries have likewise been downgraded

---

14. Sachs (1997) adheres to this view: "There is no 'fundamental' reason for Asia's financial calamity except financial panic itself." While acknowledging some vulnerabilities in the crisis countries, Radelet and Sachs (1998) also stress this theme; for example, they conclude that "The crisis is a testament to the shortcomings of international capital markets and their vulnerability to sudden reversals of market confidence."

15. See Shultz, Simon, and Wriston (1998). They conclude (A22) that "The IMF is ineffective, unnecessary and obsolete . . . Once the Asia crisis is over, we should abolish the one [IMF] we have."

sharply. What would economic growth and social stability be in these cases without any official financing?

The cushioning provided by official financing has to be accompanied by policy changes and reforms if the crisis is to be overcome. Who should administer that conditionality? Should it be administered by individual creditor countries, with all the political overtones that such bilateral negotiation would involve? Or does it work better if the party on the other side of the table is an international institution with a constitutional mandate to provide conditional financing and with a governing board on which borrowing countries sit and vote on the institution's policies? As often concluded after earlier crises, if the IMF (warts and all) didn't already exist, something a lot like it would have to be created.

Yet a third complaint is that the IMF has either been too intrusive in the policies it has recommended to the crisis countries, or alternatively, that it has not been intrusive enough.[16] On the former count, it is argued that by making detailed recommendations about financial-sector reform and corporate governance, the IMF has moved away inappropriately from its mandate of balance of payments adjustment. But could market confidence and renewed access for the Asian-crisis countries be regained without these countries undertaking reform of banks, finance companies, conglomerates, and government monopolies? Could Thailand, for example, get out of its current predicament without closing insolvent finance companies and banks? Could South Korea regain the confidence of investors without altering the way in which the government, banks, and *chaebols* conduct business with one another and without reducing the extremely high debt-to-equity ratios of the *chaebols*? Could Indonesia recover without banking reform and without giving a concrete signal that it is prepared to curtail inefficient infrastructure projects and to rein in the worst cases of "crony capitalism"? When the fiscal costs of severe banking crises frequently wind up in excess of 10 percent of the crisis country's GDP, does it make sense to set fiscal policy targets without bringing financial-sector restructuring and reform into the picture?[17]

The charge that the IMF is not intrusive enough often surfaces in the debate over whether the conditionality linked to official rescue packages ought to include measures to safeguard labor standards, to protect the environment, and to prohibit abortion. As suggested by Feldstein (1998),

---

16. Feldstein (1998) has taken the too-intrusive position. He concludes that "The IMF's recent emphasis on imposing major structural and institutional reforms as opposed to focusing on balance-of-payments adjustments will have adverse consequences in both the short term and the more distant future." The view that the IMF is not intrusive enough—or is not intrusive about the right things—has been put forward by an array of groups promoting core labor standards, or environmental concerns, or antiabortion conditionality.

17. See Goldstein (1997a) for a list of the fiscal-policy costs of banking crises in emerging economies.

the test here should be whether these measures are necessary for the crisis countries to overcome their currency and banking problems. Labor and environmental standards and anti-abortion measures do not pass that test; financial-sector reforms do.[18] Proponents of the former should push their agendas primarily in other forums—not via the IMF. If the US executive director in the IMF were obligated to vote against any IMF program that did not contain conditionality dealing with labor and environmental standards and/or with anti-abortion measures, the United States would become isolated and much less influential within the IMF. This does not mean that the US government should not candidly express its views on these matters within the IMF—but such support should stop short of making these policies a part of IMF conditionality.

IMF-led rescue packages should not become a Christmas tree on which various groups (from the creditor countries) hang their favorite legislative aims. This point does not apply only to social objectives. Large creditor countries should not use such rescue packages to obtain bilateral trade and investment concessions that are not crucial to achieving the program's broader objectives. For example, while eliminating foreign-ownership restrictions on banks may be intrinsic to financing recapitalization of those institutions, lifting a trade restriction on say, car imports from one supplier, is harder to justify. Also, the more these rescue packages are loaded up with extraneous side conditions, the harder it is going to be both to conclude these agreements in a time frame relevant to crisis management and to sustain them against political attack in the program countries.

Criticism number four is that the IMF has exacerbated the Asian crisis by prescribing excessively tight monetary and fiscal policies (cum high interest rates) and by mandating the closure of some banks and finance companies.[19] Because the crisis countries did not have serious fiscal imbalances before the crisis and because bank closures can lead to a credit crunch, the IMF's recommendations have made the contraction deeper than it needed to be. Some would go further and argue that it is because of this faulty policy mix that the rescue packages have not produced a quick turnaround in currency and equity markets.

While the critics have a point, they take it too far. It is true that it is harder to implement a successful restructuring of the financial sector if growth is slow and interest rates are high. It is also true that very high interest rates (in a context of a weak banking system and/or a recession) can be ineffective in stabilizing a falling currency if market participants

---

18. Having an adequate social safety net is more likely to pass the test. This is because the absence of a safety net may prevent the necessary monetary, fiscal, exchange rate, and structural policies from being implemented long enough to be effective.

19. See Sachs (1997) and Stiglitz (1998).

are pretty sure that such rates are sustainable for only a week or two; recall, for example, Sweden's unsuccessful effort to use 500 percent overnight rates to stabilize the kroner during the 1992 ERM crisis. Likewise, a credit squeeze can prevent domestic firms from getting the working capital they need to respond to the improved export opportunities created by a depreciated exchange rate. And the solution to overcapacity in an economy is unlikely to be contractionary fiscal policy.

But there's another side to that story. When market participants lose confidence in a currency and attach a high probability to further falls, it is difficult to induce them to hold the currency without higher interest rates. For example, it took nominal interest rates of 70 to 80 percent (for 28 day cetes[20]) for several months in early 1995 to stabilize the Mexican peso.[21] Moreover, halting a free fall of the currency takes on added importance when banks or corporations in the crisis country have large foreign-currency obligations coming due in the short term. Once the currency begins to stabilize, it may be possible to bring interest rates down substantially (so that the economy does not have to deal with them for too long). Besides all this, as Krugman (1998b) notes, for countries that are seeing their exchange rates in near free fall and are practically out of reserves, there isn't much choice: raising interest rates is the only way to support the currency.[22]

The case against closing banks in crisis countries is anything but convincing. If clearly insolvent banks/thrifts are allowed to continue operations, they are likely to "gamble for resurrection" by taking on even higher risks, adding significantly to the ultimate public-sector tab. This lesson was driven home forcefully in both the US saving and loan crisis and the ongoing Japanese banking crisis, as well as in a host of developing-country cases.

Also, not all bank runs are undesirable. Informed runs, where depositors shift funds from weak to strong banks, are a desirable element of the adjustment to banking problems. Between December 1994 and March 1995 (during the "tequila effect" of the Mexican peso crisis), some 16 percent of total deposits were withdrawn from the Argentine banking system. But an analysis of those bank runs indicates that depositors did discriminate quite sharply between weak and strong banks, punishing in particular banks that did not maintain high reserve liquidity.[23] It is only

---

20. *Cetes* are treasury bonds (denominated in domestic currency) issued by the Mexican government.

21. See IMF (1997b).

22. Krugman (1998b) also derides the notion that lowering interest rates will strengthen the economy and actually cause the currency to appreciate—characterizing such a currency/interest rate Laffer Curve as "as silly as it sounds."

23. See Fernandez (1996).

when depositors and creditors run from sound banks that problems occur. And here, too, it has to be recognized that after a period when bank credit grew at an unsustainably rapid rate, some slowdown in credit expansion is to be expected; indeed, one doesn't want bank credit going to finance the same uneconomic projects that contributed to the crisis. One key to keeping a credit contraction under control is to see that relatively stronger banks have sufficient capital so that they don't need to engage in a fire sale of assets to meet regulatory capital requirements.

Like the use of interest rate policy during a crisis, the decision of how many insolvent banks to close in a crisis is a judgement call and not a foregone conclusion (with the outcome depending in good measure on how skillfully the closures are carried out). If the *IMF* made an error in closing 16 banks during its initial agreement with Indonesia, it was that it *did not close enough banks—not that it closed too many.* There were at that time over 270 banks operating in Indonesia; the 16 banks that were closed accounted for only about 5 percent of total banking assets. The trick to restoring confidence is to convince the public that all the bad banks have been resolved, and that the ones remaining open are solid.[24] In Indonesia, it is very unlikely that the first cut of bank closures took care of the bulk of the weak banks (14 more Indonesian banks were closed recently);[25] also, the prompt reopening of a closed bank owned by one of President Suharto's sons did little to buttress the claim that bank closure decisions were being made without regard to political influence.

In a study of 24 countries that experienced systemic bank restructuring, Dziobek and Pazarbasioglu (1997) found that the countries that were quickest to diagnose the problem, assess the losses, and restructure their banking systems were generally the ones experiencing the better recovery patterns from the crisis. In short, if there is an issue on bank closures, the critics seem to have gotten the argument backward.

In any event, it looks increasingly doubtful that the original targets for monetary and fiscal policy in the official rescue packages are the main reason why the market reaction to the IMF programs was initially so disappointing. Suppose, for example, that the fiscal targets in the Indonesian and South Korean programs called for a fiscal deficit of 1 percent of GDP rather than a surplus of the same amount. Would that have produced

---

24. At a recent Centre for Economic Policy Research (CEPR) conference held in February 1998 on "Financial Crises and Asia," Michael Mussa of the IMF drew the example of the United States in 1933 when President Franklin Roosevelt called a bank holiday from which 7,000 of the nation's 25,000 banks never returned. The strongest cyclical recovery in US history began a month later. See Chote (1998) for a summary of the conference themes and discussion.

25. I have been told that at the September 1997 Annual Meetings of the IMF and World Bank in Hong Kong, lists of unsound Indonesian banks were circulating widely and that such lists had many more than 16 entries.

the market confidence necessary to buoy currency and equity markets in the crisis countries? Surely not. It needs to be recognized that when a country is undertaking a wide-ranging structural reform that promises to alter the way banks, corporations, and the government have conducted business over several decades and when the implementation of that program is scheduled over a several-year period, it is going to take some time before market participants become convinced that reform efforts are "serious"—especially if there is a false start or two. In addition, the decline in currency and equity prices has been sharpest when uncertainties about the political will and ability to implement the program have been most severe (e.g., in South Korea, in the immediate run-up to the presidential election; in Thailand, prior to the change in government; and over the first four months of 1998 in Indonesia, particularly after the health of President Suharto came under question, after rumors and then confirmation of Jusuf Habibie's appointment as vice president, and after submission of a less than realistic budget.[26]

The IMF has also made it clear that it is willing to revise the monetary and fiscal targets in these programs if growth appears to be weaker than expected at the time the programs were agreed. In short, on traditional Keynesian grounds, I suspect that an easier fiscal stance would have been appropriate, but this is not the crux of the problem. Rather, it is convincing market participants both that the structural weaknesses that played such a key role in motivating the crisis have permanently changed for the better and that the overhang of short-term debt of banks and corporations can be resolved in a satisfactory and reasonably expeditious way.

The fifth criticism is one that merits the most attention, because it affects not only this crisis but the probability of getting into similar financial crises in the future. It goes under the broad heading of *moral hazard problems*, that is, the provision of insurance by the official sector that acts as a subsidy to risk taking and, thus, results in too many resources being channeled into the insured activities.

After the Mexican crisis, the G-10 countries undertook a review of how to deal with sovereign liquidity crises (G-10 1996; executive summary reprinted in Kenen 1996). The emphasis was on sovereign liquidity crises, because Mexico's debt crisis involved sovereign bonds and because it was implicitly assumed that private-sector debt rescheduling presented fewer unresolved problems than did rescheduling of sovereign debt.

Among the relevant conclusions of the G-10 report, the following merit explicit mention (Kenen 1996, 74–75): (1) " [N]either debtor countries nor their creditors should expect to be insulated from adverse financial consequences by the provision of large-scale official financing in the event of a crisis;" (2) "[T]here should be no presumption that any type of debt

---

26. See Ito (1998c) on these political factors in the crisis countries.

will be exempt from payments suspensions or restructurings in the event of a future sovereign liquidity crisis;" and (3) "[N]ote was taken of the current policies of the IMF that provide, under exceptional circumstances, for lending in support of effective adjustment programmes prior to full and final resolution of the sovereign borrowers' arrears to private creditors. It would be advisable for the IMF Executive Board to review existing policy in this area and to consider whether the scope of its application should be extended to other forms of debt not covered." In identifying a broad set of principles and features that should guide the resolution of future sovereign liquidity crises, the report also urged: "I[I]t should minimize moral hazard for both creditors and debtors;" and *it should strengthen the ability of governments to resist pressures to assume responsibility for the external liabilities of their private sectors"* [emphasis added].

One might then ask: well, if these were the principles that were to guide the (post-Mexico) resolution of future liquidity crises and if the Thai, Indonesian, and South Korean crises dealt primarily with private debt (rather than the tougher case of sovereign debt), how did the United States wind up with nearly $120 billion in official rescue packages—particularly since US Treasury Secretary Rubin has indicated on a number of occasions that he wouldn't be willing to "spend a nickel" on bailing out private creditors?

To be fair, several things should be recognized at the outset. First, the rescue packages go primarily for purposes other than to prevent rescheduling of debt to private creditors; namely, they go to cushion the (inevitable) recession in the crisis countries, to help to rebuild international reserves, and to help to recapitalize the banking system. As noted above, I would argue that these are indeed legitimate uses of IMF resources. Second, in at least the Thai and Indonesian cases, the IMF probably acted in the direction of restraining national authorities in the crisis countries from engaging in even larger bailouts of large, uninsured creditors of banks and corporations. For example, the Thai authorities announced a blanket guarantee for depositors and creditors of Thai banks and finance companies. After 58 finance companies were closed in Thailand, the original (Thai) plan was to give the large creditors of these finance companies bonds at market interest rates in exchange for their existing claims; the IMF apparently fought successfully to make these bonds carry a below-market rate of return (2 percent)—so that large creditors took a nontrivial hit. Similarly, I understand that language was written into the Indonesian program to try to limit the diversion of IMF funds for bailing out the creditors of large corporations. Third, there is a good case for bailing out small retail depositors of banks (because they are apt to be less sophisticated and efficient at judging the soundness of banks).[27] Fourth, through-

27. See Benston and Kaufman (1988).

out the crisis, equity holders and bond holders have "taken a hit." It is probably the case that they would have taken even a bigger hit without IMF involvement, but they certainly have paid a significant penalty. The main problem is with large, uninsured creditors of banks.[28]

IMF/G-10 attitudes seem to have shifted by the time of the South Korean rescue. By that time, the depth and contagion of the Asian crisis were more serious. Also, as in the Thai case, the South Korean authorities, in an effort to stem the crisis, had indicated (in August 1997) that they were prepared to guarantee the liabilities of all South Korean financial institutions and overseas subsidiaries.[29] Presumably, a decision was made that attempting to reschedule the short-term debts of South Korean banks (that is, impose a hit on the creditors of these banks) would risk spreading the crisis further. Perhaps there was also a concern that there was no easy way to do this in a nonconfrontational way, without going the full monty of a "debt moratorium." By late December 1997, when a short-term rescheduling (default) on South Korean debt was closer at hand, the official sector was apparently even more concerned about the spillover effects of a rescheduling on South Korean bank debt and opted to increase the speed of official disbursements and to lean on bank creditors to roll over the debt coming due over the next month.

While none of us can confidently know the counterfactual, I would argue that the decision *not* to rely more heavily on rescheduling of short-term bank debt in December 1997 was a mistake and, in concert with mega-IMF rescue packages, risks sending us down the road to an approach to crisis management that cannot be sustained.[30] My view rests on the following arguments.

Operating exclusively on the borrower to limit moral hazard is not apt to be effective. In this connection, two characterizations of the cost of borrowing from the IMF have often been advanced over the past few years. Neither of them is correct.

The first characterization is that the IMF lends money to countries at highly subsidized rates, thereby encouraging these borrowers to under-

---

28. Commercial bank lending is an important component of net private capital flows to Asia. According to the IMF (1998b), commercial banks accounted for about one-third of net private capital flows to developing countries in Asia during the 1990s—versus about one-fifth for all developing countries.

29. Given that the market knew by this time that South Korean reserves were small relative to these liabilities, it can be argued that this announcement led to a rush for the door; see the discussion in Chote (1998).

30. Volcker (1997, 11) also seems to regard the frequency and size of recent official rescue packages with concern: "I can well understand and sympathize with the instinct of the official community to provide prompt assistance to bridge the external financing gap. At the same time the increased frequency and size of those rescue packages raise more insistently questions about their sustainability and long-term effectiveness. . . . [T]here is a striking

Table 13   Use of IMF credit (millions of SDRs), 1995-97

	1995	1996	1997
General resources account	16,967.92	5,270.96	16,112.86
Standby arrangements	14,382.11ª	2,471.06	13,255.39
Of which: Supplemental reserve facility	na	na	4,100.00
EFF arrangements	1,965.16	2,625.29	2,749.87
CCFF	8.93	174.62	107.60
STF	611.73	na	na
SAF and ESAF arrangements	1,431.44	708.64	730.59
Total	18,399.36	5,979.60	16,843.45

CCFF = Compensatory and contingency financing facility
EFF = Extended fund facility
ESAF = Enhanced structural adjustment facility
na = not applicable
SAF = Structural adjustment facility
STF = Systemic transformation facility

Note: Figures may not add up to totals shown due to rounding.

a. Includes credit tranche of SDR 651.7 million purchased by Zambia on 6 December 1995, which was subsequently repurchased on 18 December 1995 following disbursement from the ESAF Trust.

Source: IMF, *IMF Survey* 27, no. 3 (9 February 1998): 34; IMF Treasury Department.

take excessive risk taking.[31] Indeed, one proposed bill in the US House of Representatives would compel the IMF to offer loans at rates "comparable" to those in private financial markets (adjusted for risk).

The interest rate that countries pay for borrowing from the IMF depends on which borrowing facility (facilities) they make use of. While the IMF operates one significant concessional facility, the Enhanced Structural Adjustment Facility (with an interest rate of 0.5 percent per year and repayments that begin 5.5 years after and end 10 years after the date of each disbursement), the facilities most relevant for situations akin to the Asian crisis are the IMF's regular facilities (standby arrangements and the Extended Fund Facility [EFF] arrangements) and the newly created Supplemental Reserve Facility (SRF). As shown in table 13, about 90 percent of the use of IMF credit in 1997 was accounted for by its regular facilities.

Countries that enter into standby and EFF arrangements with the IMF pay an interest rate (called the rate of charge) that is a weighted average of the short-term interest rates in the G-5 countries (where the weights are the same as those used to construct the Special Drawing Rights [SDRs]),

---

difference between the financial crises of the 1990s and the Latin American debt crisis of the 1980s. Much more limited official assistance was forthcoming in the earlier episode."

31. See Armey (1998) and Calomiris (1998).

plus a small surcharge.[32] Reflecting the fact that G-5 interest rates (particularly in Japan) have recently been unusually low, the rate of charge averaged 4.7 percent in 1997.[33] The SRF was put in place in December 1997. It aims "to provide financial assistance to a member country experiencing exceptional balance of payments difficulties due to a large short-term financing need resulting from the sudden disruptive loss of market confidence reflected in pressure on the capital account and the member's reserves."[34] With the SRF, there is an expectation that the correction in the balance of payments can be accomplished within a short period of time. As such, repayment periods under the SRF will normally be one to one-and-a-half years after the date of each disbursement; also, during the first year of the loan, SRF borrowers will pay an interest rate of 300 basis points above the rate of charge on regular IMF loans, and this will increase by 50 basis points at the end of that period and every six months thereafter until the surcharge reaches 500 basis points.[35] South Korea was the first country (in December 1997) to draw on the SRF, receiving SDR4.1 billion (roughly $5.5 billion) of the total amount of SDR15.5 billion (roughly $21 billion) approved under the standby arrangement.

Because developing countries—especially when they are encountering difficulties—cannot access international financial markets on terms that are nearly as favorable as those available to the G-5 countries, it is certainly accurate to say that such countries pay interest rates on their borrowings from the IMF that are lower than they might obtain from the markets. Cline and Barnes (1997), for example, calculate that average eurobond spreads (relative to US Treasury bonds) for 11 major emerging market economies ranged from 315 basis points in late 1995 to 118 basis points in September 1997, before rising to 230 basis points at the end of October. Radelet and Sachs (1997) report that the spread on Thai sovereign bonds was 39 basis points in the second quarter of 1996 and was still only 79 basis points in August, a month after the crisis had begun. In early April 1998, South Korea placed 5-year bonds (cum a government guarantee for

---

32. These weights are as follows: United States, 43 percent; France, 10 percent; Germany, 17 percent; Japan, 17 percent; and the United Kingdom, 13 percent. Standby arrangements cover a one to three year period, drawings are normally phased in on a quarterly basis, and repayments are made within 3.25 to 5 years of each drawing. EFF arrangements normally run for three years (and can be extended for a fourth), have phasing comparable to those of standby arrangements, and repayments are made within 4.5 to 10 years of the drawing. EFF arrangements are designed to remedy balance of payments problems that originate largely from structural problems and require a longer period of adjustment; they generally also provide larger amounts of financing than standby arrangements.

33. See IMF (1998c).

34. See IMF (1998c).

35. See IMF (1998c).

a few those years) at a spread of 345 basis points above US Treasury bonds and 10-year bonds at 355 basis points.[36]

One has to be careful, however, not to compare apples with oranges. The big difference between IMF (upper-credit tranche) programs and loans from the private sector is that the former always come with strong policy conditionality. As noted above, the IMF-led rescue packages with Thailand, Indonesia, and South Korea, in addition to conditions on monetary, fiscal, and exchange rate policies, carried a large helping of structural policy commitments, especially in the financial sector. From the point of view of the national policymaker, a loan agreement that strongly circumscribes his/her room for maneuver—and that might be used by political opponents to argue that the national authorities have surrendered the steering wheel to foreigners—is likely to be viewed as more "costly" than one that does not carry such conditionality.[37] In other words, when valuing the cost of borrowing from the IMF, one ought to think in terms of the conditionality-equivalent interest rate, not just the nominal interest rate on the loan—the former will be higher than the latter. In fact, if IMF loans carried the huge subsidy that many of the IMF's critics claim, then one would expect to see countries tripping over themselves in a rush to come to the IMF as soon there was a balance of payments need and *before* they turned to (higher-cost) private lenders. But this is exactly the opposite of what we in fact observe. Countries with serious payments problems usually come to the IMF *late* in the game, after their external problems are quite severe and only after they've exhausted their access to other lenders. The recent behavior of the Thai, Indonesian, and South Korean authorities in the run-up to the Asian financial crisis is a case in point. All of this should send a signal that one cannot easily capture any subsidy associated with IMF borrowing by reference to a simple interest rate comparison of IMF programs and loans/bonds from private creditors.

The second characterization is that the cost of IMF borrowing—inclusive of the costs of IMF conditionality—are so high as to deter sovereign borrowers from counting on the IMF as a backstop in case of a crisis. For example, it was sometimes said that after the costs Mexico incurred during the peso crisis, no rational borrower would allow itself to get into that kind of trouble again. Clearly, whatever the costs and coinsurance associated with IMF policy conditionality, the demonstration effect of Mexico was not sufficient to deter overborrowing in Southeast Asia and South Korea (as indicated in chapter 2).

---

36. See JP Morgan Securities, cited in *New York Times*, 9 April 1998.

37. To take but one recent example, when South Korea signed its standby arrangement with the IMF in December 1997, some South Korean opposition leaders referred to it as a "day of national humiliation." Loans obtained from the private capital markets are not described in such terms, although it is clear that private capital markets also force policy changes on errant sovereign borrowers.

In my view, a better approach to reducing moral hazard in IMF-led official rescue packages would be to operate also on private lenders. Specifically, the only thing that will deter their excessive risk taking is a nontrivial probability of incurring a significant loss, which in turn requires that they occasionally actually *do* suffer a loss.

If the G-10 and the IMF want their pronouncements on official bailouts to be credible—particularly in the wake of the bail out of *tesobono*[38] holders in Mexico—they need to act in accord with those pronouncements when push comes to shove in a crisis. The efforts that went into avoiding an earlier rescheduling of the debts of insolvent South Korean banks seem inconsistent with the principles laid out in the G-10 report (as cited above). Clearly, if the official safety net becomes wider and wider over time (based on the case law of actual rescues), we can expect private lenders to increasingly channel international capital flows into the debts of those borrowers and lenders who are deemed "too large to fail"—no matter what G-10 reports say. What sense then will it make to complain about excessively narrow spreads on emerging-market paper (especially bank debt) and to emphasize repeatedly in official reports that the first line of defense against crises is good risk management by banks and corporations if the official sector "blinks" whenever a large borrower is in trouble?

It is not obvious that a rescheduling of South Korean bank debt could not have been undertaken earlier on in the crisis without exacerbating it; nor is it clear that the first round of rollovers that did take place (in New York, Frankfurt, and Tokyo) would not have happened anyway in the absence of a promise of accelerated disbursements from the official sector. The argument that creditors are too numerous and disbursed to make such discussions feasible did not seem to apply in this case. If the rescue package for South Korea were smaller (say, $30 billion instead of $58 billion) and disbursements were not accelerated, a larger amount would have had to be rescheduled. But it is not clear why the smaller amount is to be preferred to a larger one. After all, this is private bank debt and the lenders have been compensated with risk premiums that reflected some probability of nonrepayment. In contrast to the 1982 situation, US and European banks were not in danger of being made insolvent by a hit on their loans to Asia. Admittedly, taking such a hit would have been a bigger problem for Japanese banks, but a large public injection is already needed there (see discussion above) and the Japanese economy is rich enough to afford it. Yes, there could have been larger spillovers to other emerging-market borrowers, but the IMF could have been prepared to extend liquidity to those countries whose solvent banks were adversely affected by South Korean rescheduling. Moreover, the G-10 report cited above spoke approvingly of the IMF's "lending into arrears" policy, at

---

38. *Tesobonos* are US dollar indexed treasury bonds issued by the Mexican government.

least for extreme circumstances. So long as South Korea was carrying out its adjustment program and bargaining in good faith with its private creditors, why was an acceleration of disbursements crucial? And if South Korea can obtain an acceleration of official disbursements (before meeting the earlier agreed on performance criteria), what will be the message to banks, corporations, and national governments in other emerging economies? In the end, it's possible that moving ahead with a nonconfrontational rescheduling of private bank debt (in which the official sector lends its good offices to the proceedings but doesn't rush in with additional funds) may be less anxiety raising than making a sharp zero-one distinction between default and rescheduling. Little of what went on in debt negotiations involving South Korean banks was totally voluntary anyway—as officials leaned on their banks to undertake the initial one-month rollover. Nor is the oft-made distinction between illiquidity and insolvency so clear-cut here either. I suspect that many crisis-country banks were insolvent even if their assets and liabilities were marked to market at precrisis prices.

Bailing out large uninsured creditors of private banks also makes it harder to sell the principle of *equitable burden sharing*. Because of the expected contraction of economic activity and the higher cost of living, ordinary citizens in the crisis countries will need to make substantial sacrifices to overcome the crisis. It will be harder to convince them to do so if large lenders (domestic and foreign) escape their share of the burden. Similarly, if the IMF and the G-10 wish to maintain support for the funding of these packages, G-10 countries should not put their legislators in the position of trying to justify an outcome where governments put up the funds but a certain class of private investors (who made bad lending decisions) walks away whole.

Fortunately, there are policy and institutional changes that can be implemented to reduce (albeit not eliminate) the moral hazard associated with official rescue packages. These are best discussed, however, within the broader context of efforts to improve the international framework for crisis prevention and crisis management, to which we turn next.

4

Halifax II Reforms

There is nothing like a crisis to motivate a rethink of the adequacy of the existing crisis prevention/management architecture. In this sense, the Mexican peso crisis helped to motivate progress on, inter alia, an international data standard (the IMF's Special Data Dissemination Standard [SDDS]), an international banking standard (the Core Principles), an Emergency Financing Mechanism in the IMF, and expanding the credit facilities available to the IMF under the New Arrangements to Borrow.[1] In a similar way, the Asian financial crisis is already motivating—and will continue to motivate over the next few years—discussions about how to reform the international financial architecture. As these Halifax II discussions proceed, the following five issues ought to receive priority: (1) reducing moral hazard and making private debt rescheduling more orderly and more flexible; (2) strengthening prudential standards in developing countries and making it more attractive for countries to implement these standards sooner; (3) improving transparency and disclosure in financial markets; (4) giving IMF surveillance more punch; and (5) shoring up risk management in global financial institutions.[2] I turn next to each of these issues.

---

1. See Summers (1996).

2. Some would even go farther and add a review of G-3 exchange rate policy to the agenda. I have given my thoughts on what could realistically be done in this area in Goldstein (1995). Volcker (1997) offers another view on this matter.

Moral Hazard and Debt Rescheduling

Finding a *way to reduce moral hazard and to make the rescheduling of private external debt more orderly* should top the agenda. Because these moral hazard and rescheduling issues were not well thought out prior to the current crisis, official rescue packages turned out to be much larger than anyone anticipated, with longer-run moral hazard effects being held hostage to short-term (but admittedly important) financial stability concerns. Although bank debt starts out in the private sector, it often winds up in the official sector, bringing with it all the problems associated with rescheduling sovereign debt. It is not inevitable that such official rescue efforts result in certain private lenders escaping their fair share of the adjustment burden.

One step in a helpful direction would be to seek *international agreement* that in future IMF-led rescue packages that involve restructuring of the financial sector, *governments cannot expect "blanket-guarantee announcements" (issued before the IMF arrives on the scene) to be honored.* As noted above, such blanket guarantee statements were issued by both the Thai and South Korean authorities. Once such statements are made, they place the IMF and creditor countries in a bind. If the guarantees are honored, then the case history of official bailouts gets another entry, and it becomes that much more difficult to convince private creditors that "next time things will be different." On the other hand, if the guarantee statement is rescinded, it reduces the credibility of national authorities when that credibility is important for convincing the market that their future statements will be honored. The answer is to obtain international agreement that the treatment of large, uninsured creditors of private firms (including banks) is part and parcel of the conditionality associated with such programs and that the scope and duration of any guarantees (that extend beyond small depositors of banks) are to be negotiated with the IMF.

A second key step is to encourage emerging economies to *adopt a system of deposit insurance that is incentive compatible and that places large, uninsured creditors of banks in the back of the queue when failed banks are resolved.* In this connection, there is a good deal that can be exported from the features contained in recent US banking legislation, namely, the Federal Deposit Insurance Corporation Improvement Act (FDICIA) of 1991.[3]

Several features of FDICIA are relevant for how emerging market economies should design their official safety nets. For one, FDICIA retains deposit insurance for small depositors (up to a maximum of $100,000 per depositor).[4] The rationale for such insurance is that it is small retail

---

3. For a comprehensive discussion of the rationale for FDICIA, as well as for a review of its performance, see Benston and Kaufman (1988, 1997) and Feldman and Rolnick (1998).

4. FDICIA also specifies that the deposit-insurance premiums paid by banks be risk weighted (depending on their capital and bank examination ratings), although debate continues on

depositors who are least likely to be able to ascertain the true financial condition of banks and thus who are most likely to engage in *uninformed* bank runs. It might also be said that because such small depositors are so numerous, they are likely to have enough political clout to get paid off after a crisis anyway, and deposit insurance at least sets out a maximum on that payout. According to a 1996 survey by Garcia and Lindgren (1996), only about 50 of the IMF's 180 member countries had explicit deposit-insurance systems in place (see table 14), and even among those countries that had such systems, departures from best practice were common.[5]

Even more to the issue at hand, FDICIA makes it harder for regulators to bail out large uninsured creditors of banks. Specifically, FDICIA requires that the FDIC evaluate all possible resolution alternatives and pick the one that carries the lowest cost to the deposit-insurance fund (so-called "least cost resolution"). There is a discretionary systemic override provision to fully protect all bank creditors in exceptional circumstances (that is, in banks deemed "too big to fail"), but that override requires the explicit consent of the secretary of the treasury in consultation with the president of the United States, two thirds of the governors of the Federal Reserve System, and two thirds of the directors of the FDIC. While FDICIA has not been in effect long enough to fully test its mettle, the preliminary evidence is encouraging in the sense that the coverage of uninsured depositors at failed banks has been much lower post-FDICIA (1992–96) than it was pre-FDICIA (1986–1991); see figure 1, taken from Feldman and Rolnick (1998).

Other features of FDICIA worth mentioning are that banks become subject to progressively harsher regulatory sanctions as their capital falls below multiple capital-zone trip wires (so-called "prompt corrective action"), well-capitalized banks receive "carrots" in the form of greater banking powers and lighter regulatory oversight, and there is an explicit exit rule for banks that calls for closure of a bank while it still has positive net worth.

Some have argued that with consolidation producing more and more large banks, even FDICIA doesn't go far enough in mandating that large uninsured creditors of failed banks take a haircut. Feldman and Rolnick

---

whether the differences across banks in these risk weights are sharp enough (see Benston and Kaufman 1988, 1997). Other countries with risk-adjusted deposit-insurance premiums include Argentina, Portugal, and Sweden (see Garcia 1998).

5. Garcia (1998) provides a listing of best practice for deposit insurance systems. In addition to avoiding incentive problems, her list includes, inter alia: laying out the system explicitly in law and regulation; providing the banking supervisor with a system of prompt remedial actions; resolving failed depository institutions promptly; keeping insurance coverage reasonably low (e.g., not in excess of one to two times per capita GDP); making membership compulsory (to avoid adverse selection problems); paying out insured deposits quickly; charging risk-adjusted insurance premiums; and ensuring that the deposit insurance agency is independent.

Table 14 Countries with explicit deposit insurance systems

Africa (4)	Asia (7)	Europe (23)		Middle East (4)	Western Hemisphere (12)
Kenya	Bangladesh	Austria	Italy	Bahrain	Argentina
Nigeria	India	Belgium	Luxembourg	Kuwait	Brazil
Tanzania	Japan	Bulgaria	Netherlands	Lebanon	Canada
Uganda	Marshall Islands	Czech Republic	Norway	Oman	Chile
	Micronesia	Denmark	Poland		Colombia
	Philippines	Finland	Portugal		Dominican Republic
	Taiwan	France	Spain		El Salvador
		Germany	Sweden		Mexico
		Greece	Switzerland		Peru
		Hungary	Turkey		Trinidad and Tobago
		Iceland	United Kingdom		United States
		Ireland			Venezuela

Source: Garcia (1998).

Figure 1   Failed commercial banks by uninsured depositor treatment, 1986-96

percentages

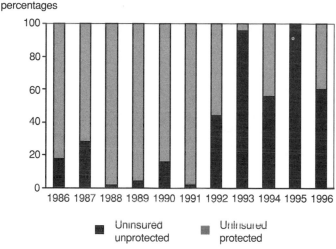

Source: Federal Reserve Bank of Minneapolis, 1997 Annual Report; Federal Deposit Insurance Corporation.

(1998), for example, have argued that FDICIA should be amended to guarantee that uninsured depositors cannot be fully protected when "too big to fail" is invoked. This could be implemented by specifying that uninsured depositors experience a threshold loss before they receive any protection (e.g., 20 percent of their uninsured deposits).[6] In addition to "coinsurance" of losses at too-big-to-fail banks, Feldman and Rolnick (1998) propose that deposit-insurance premiums paid by banks incorporate the risk premiums that depositors and other creditors receive in the market on their uninsured funds and that the regulators require the disclosure of additional data (e.g., on loans with late repayments) on banks' financial condition.

I am not suggesting that emerging economies copy exactly the US model. But they do need some type of (preagreed) mechanism that creates a strong presumption that when serious banking difficulties erupt, large uninsured creditors are going to be placed in the back of the queue, and that when they are protected during truly exceptional circumstances, there will be stringent accountability and transparency conditions on the part of the most senior economic officials. The point is not to ignore legitimate concerns about systemic stability but rather to reach a better compromise between the tools that will be available (to firefighters) for putting out

---

6. Reflecting wider systemic concerns, Feldman and Rolnick (1998) also argue for a "cap" and a "floor" to these losses for uninsured depositors at too-big-to-fail banks.

the current fire and the incentives needed to make the next set of fires smaller and less likely.

Step number three goes in a similar direction of *limiting the scope and duration of the official safety net.* The rationale for official liquidity support of financial institutions rests on a difference between social and private returns. The social return to rescuing finance companies and merchant banks will normally be weaker than that for rescuing banks. The former, for example, are not usually involved in the operation of the payments system; moreover, they often become a vehicle in emerging markets for engaging heavily in higher-risk activities because of their lighter regulatory burden vis-à-vis banks. Just as uninsured wholesale creditors should normally be expected to take a larger hit than insured retail depositors during a crisis, there should be an *agreement that countries receiving official rescue packages will not extend protection to finance companies and merchant banks.* Extending the same line of argument, the official safety net should not encompass nonfinancial corporations.

Much in the same spirit of limiting inappropriate extension of the safety net, in cases where countries do decide to provide guarantees to banks during a crisis (the above arguments notwithstanding), there should be a presumption that *any guarantees will carry a strict time limit, say, no more than one year.* Again, there may be individual-country circumstances where exceptions to this presumption can be justified—but the burden of proof ought to be placed on the borrowing country to convince official lenders of the exceptional nature of its predicament. All guarantees should not be regarded equally: long-running ones should be subject to even greater scrutiny than triage operations.

Yet a fourth helpful step would be to *bring more order and flexibility into the rescheduling of private external debt.* One of the important lessons of the 1980s debt crisis is that long delays in reducing a large debt overhang (that is unlikely to be paid in full anyway) can seriously exacerbate the effects of the crisis on the real economy.[7]

To bring greater order into the debt rescheduling process, governments (as well as large financial firms) should make it their responsibility to have comprehensive and up-to-date figures on the size and composition of external debt, along with the identity and concentration of major creditors. Rescheduling operations cannot proceed efficiently if there is a weak factual basis to evaluate the size of the debt burden and the extent of the cash-flow problem and if there is uncertainty about the practicality of drawing the major creditors together for a discussion. As noted later in this chapter, the incentive to collect and maintain such data can be increased by strengthening the IMF's SDDS.

---

7. See Corden and Dooley (1989). Cline (1995) is more skeptical about the size of any debt overhang effects on the real economy.

Beyond this, the orderliness of private debt rescheduling would be well served by promoting better organization of creditors in advance, and by making adaptations to debt contracts that can help overcome collective action problems. Specifically, there is merit in the proposals put forward by Eichengreen and Portes (1995, 1998) to have *standing steering committees for bond holders and to include sharing clauses and majority voting clauses in these debt instruments*. The idea here is to avoid the costs and delays of organizing creditors on the spot and to make it more difficult for rogue creditors to block rescheduling efforts.

In the G-10 report (1996), the official sector expressed some support for adaptation of debt instruments but would not go so far as setting an example by including majority voting provisions in its own sovereign bond contracts. It preferred instead to wait for the market to lead the way. But as noted earlier (Eichengreen and Portes 1996; Goldstein 1996), this market-led adoption may never come if only bond contracts of less creditworthy borrowers contain such clauses. For in that case, the very presence of the clause may be taken by the market as a signal of a greater intention to renegotiate. In view of the importance of debt rescheduling in the Asian crisis, the G-10 ought to reexamine its earlier position, eliminate the adverse signaling problem, and lead the way by incorporating desirable innovations in its own instruments.

In terms of enhancing the flexibility of debt rescheduling and encouraging private creditors to assume their fair share of the adjustment burden, here too there are helpful changes that can be made at the margin. For the most part, these involve the *official sector in the major creditor countries making it clearer that it will adopt a more benign view of informal debt standstills, of early proposals for debt-for-debt and equity-for-debt exchanges by the debtor, and of IMF "lending into arrears"—so long as these measures are confined to cases where the debtor is truly laboring under a crisis situation cum an unsustainable debt burden and where the debtor has negotiated in good faith with its private creditors*.[8] In the case of IMF lending into arrears, the debtor country

---

8. A policy of having the IMF lend into arrears on private debt does not just affect the balance of power between debtors and creditors in the debt negotiation. It also provides important "debtor in possession" financing for the debtor country; see Calvo and Goldstein (1996). The view of G-7 governments on debt negotiations between debtors from developing countries and financial institutions from G-7 countries can have important effects on the outcome of these negotiations. An outstanding example was the impetus given to debt reduction in the 1980s when the G-7 switched from the Baker Plan to the Brady Plan (see Cline 1995).

As an example of such a flexible approach to rescheduling of private debt, Litan (1998) has proposed a strategy of triage, liquidation, and workouts to handle the private debt overhang in the Asian crisis countries. The first step would be to have each country establish a mechanism for performing triage on all firms and banks facing bankruptcy, using an exchange rate below the precrisis level but above current, excessively depressed market levels. Step two would be to subject all firms and banks that are insolvent under this exchange rate by some threshold margin to a presumption of liquidation or forced merger,

should also of course be meeting its policy commitments under an IMF program. Where decent national bankruptcy laws don't exist, the general stance of the IMF and G-7 governments should be not to oppose ad hoc debt-negotiation proceedings and outcomes that mimic what might be expected to have taken place if such bankruptcy laws were in place.

The intention here is not for the official sector to encourage private debtors to walk away from their contractual obligations at the first hint of trouble. It is rather for the official sector to set itself a higher systemic-risk threshold before it intervenes (with additional liquidity support) as a substitute for beginning debt rescheduling negotiations between private debtors and private creditors. If the official sector in the G-10 countries alternatively sends a signal that such reschedulings and IMF lending into arrears are options that need to be avoided at almost all cost (because, say, of the perceived danger of contagion), then it will be hard to convince private creditors that it is in their interest to push for a prompt resolution. In other words, private debt reschedulings need to be accepted more readily by the official sector as a normal response to truly abnormal circumstances; otherwise, there will be little alternative to placing too much of the adjustment burden on all parties other than private creditors.

This view would not preclude the official sector (both national governments and the international financing institutions [IFIs]) from acting as an "honest broker" if a large share of the banking system or the corporate sector is facing liquidity/solvency problems. In this role, the official sector could assist the negotiating parties in bringing together the necessary factual data, provide an objective assessment of the likely impact on the economy of various debt rescheduling options, and try to keep the discussions from becoming too confrontational.

To sum up, finding a more orderly and flexible approach to the rescheduling of private external debt is the only way to get back to a situation where official rescue packages are of a reasonable size and where market discipline operates across a broader spectrum of emerging-market financial instruments. Such an approach does entail the risk that, once started, crises may be harder to manage than when large-scale bailouts and guarantees are a large part of the arsenal. But that is the risk that has to be taken to limit incentives that would otherwise increase the likelihood of more and larger crises in the future. The reality is that the Asian crisis will not be resolved until the heavy short-term debt burden of banks and

---

unless creditors quickly accept an equity-for-debt swap. And step three would be to make all insolvent firms and banks not subject to liquidation (or below regulatory capital standards) eligible for Chapter 11-type workouts, with lenders required to exchange some portion of debt for equity. Foreign banks would automatically take haircuts. In lieu of a equity-for-debt exchange, governments would only extend guarantees on loans once they've been partially forgiven. Litan (1998, 8) concludes that such an active liquidation and workout plan "would send a message to all creditors that the days of too big to fail are over and that pain must be widely shared if all are to feel comfortable with the outcome."

corporations in the crisis countries is rescheduled or turned into equity. The sooner creditors accept that reality, the better.

Prudential/Supervisory Standards

A second key item on the Halifax II agenda should be *strengthening prudential/supervisory standards in emerging economies and improving the incentives for their early adoption.* Because banking crises in emerging economies have been so frequent and so costly over the past 15 years and because banks account for the lion's share of financial assets in these economies, the emphasis should be on moving more countries more quickly toward an international banking standard.[9]

In September 1997, at the Annual Meeting of the IMF and World Bank group in Hong Kong, agreement was reached on the Core Principles (Basle Committee on Banking Supervision 1997). Warts and all, the Core Principles represent a welcome and significant advance on what existed before in international banking supervision. Previous agreements had a narrow scope, that is, they were pretty much restricted to defining regulatory bank capital and to encouraging better cooperation between home- and host-country bank supervisors.[10] The Core Principles are much more comprehensive and address many of the problems that had plagued, and still continue to plague, banking supervision in developing countries. Over the next six months to a year, attention should be directed to two sets of initiatives: making it more attractive for countries to publicly sign on the Core Principles and improving the content of the Core Principles themselves.

While last September's agreement on the Core Principles urged countries to make public their intention to implement this voluntary international banking standard, the agreement unfortunately did not contain a target date for such participation. This was a mistake that should now be rectified. *A target date (for announcing who is and is not complying with the standard) is essential to help to motivate the implementation of the Core Principles.* Ask yourself: how far would the EU countries have come on fiscal consolidation without the spur that entry decisions would be taken by a date certain, namely, early 1998? Similarly, would APEC's 1994 pledge to achieve "free and open trade and investment in the region" have credibility without an explicit 2010 date for industrial countries and a 2020 date for the others?[11] Or, to take an even closer example, why does

---

9. See Goldstein (1997a; 1997b) and Goldstein and Turner (1996).

10. See Goldstein (1997a) for a fuller discussion and critique of previous international banking agreements.

11. See Bergsten (1996).

the IMF's SDDS carry a cut-off date by which countries have to announce their adherence to the standard? The answer is that a target date serves as an action-enforcing mechanism for getting policymakers to take their commitment seriously. In this respect, the Core Principles are no different than other international or regional agreements. Given the magnitude of the task ahead in many developing countries to meet the conditions for the Core Principles, it would in my view be reasonable to set a five-year-hence target date (2003 or so). Some may prefer a slightly shorter or longer target date. But a date certain is a must.

Two other initiatives would reinforce the incentives countries have to sign on to the Core Principles. One would be to *strengthen the mandate that the IMF and the World Bank have in monitoring countries' compliance with the Core Principles*. Because participation is voluntary, the main payoff from participating in the standard is the market payoff (that is, a lower risk premium) attached to having the authorities certify that banking supervision in a country meets minimum international standards. We cannot rely on the national banking supervisor alone to render that judgement because a weak and nonindependent supervisory authority is part of the problem in many developing countries. Having an international agency evaluate compliance with the Core Principles will carry more credibility than evaluation done exclusively by national banking authorities.[12]

Admittedly, the expertise of the IMF and the World Bank on banking supervision is not as deep and broad as it is in their more traditional areas of specialization. Nevertheless, they both have experienced staff in the banking area, and efforts to recruit and train more experts are reportedly moving ahead full steam. Also, an effective monitoring job requires ground troops cum on-site visits, and the Bretton Woods twins are the only IFIs that have enough ground troops to do the job.[13] Over time, it may be that the private rating agencies will see it in their interest to make compliance with international banking standards a regular part of their sovereign risk analysis—but for now, we have to rely on the IMF and the World Bank to get the ball rolling.

As of late, there has been active debate on a proposed amendment to the IMF's Articles of Agreement that would make capital account liberalization a purpose of the IMF and that would extend the IMF's jurisdiction to capital movements.[14] In my view, a better tack—if one wants any major expansion of IMF activities to be anchored in the IMF's articles—would be to make financial stability (rather than capital account

---

12. See Goldstein (1997a, 1997b).

13. The BIS has significant expertise in banking and banking supervision matters but its staff is far too small to take on a monitoring task of this scale.

14. See Fischer (1997).

liberalization) the focus of an amendment.[15] I say this for two reasons. The first is that there is greater consensus on the need for developing countries to establish a strong supervisory and prudential framework than there is on the wisdom of pushing ahead with capital account liberalization. For example, you don't hear of emerging economies who allegedly fared better during 1997 because they weakened their systems of banking supervision. Second, it is becoming widely accepted that inadequate preparation is the main reason why some many financial crises in developing countries have been preceded by capital account liberalization, and establishing a sound supervisory framework is probably the single most important element of that preparation.[16] In other words, a financial stability element, in addition to its own merits, would contribute to advancing the long-run goal of capital account convertibility while avoiding many of the operational pitfalls associated with a capital account amendment (for example, permitting or even counseling developing countries facing large capital inflows to consider adopting "Chile-type" taxes on short-term capital inflows—at the same time that these countries are being asked to move in the longer term toward dismantling capital restrictions).

In addition to the market payoff, *a second incentive* to sign on to the Core Principles could be linked to *larger access to IMF and World Bank loans*. As suggested in Calvo and Goldstein (1996), the IMF and the World Bank could make the degree of access to their resources more dependent on the crisis-preventive measures taken by countries, including their adherence to international banking and data disclosure standards.[17] Countries that did less to reduce their vulnerability would still be able to draw, but their access lines would be smaller. This would help to reduce moral hazard on the borrower's side from IMF-led rescue packages.

So much for the incentives to upgrade supervisory and prudential standards in emerging economies. Progress would also be furthered by *sharpening and extending the content of the Core Principles in three directions*.

For one thing, the Core Principles should set out a *tougher line on greater transparency for government involvement in the banking system*. It's not adequate simply to say that state-owned banks should be subject to

---

15. It is my understanding that the April 1998 meeting of the IMF's Interim Committee took up this issue.

16. See Kaminsky and Reinhart (1996) on the statistical link between banking crises and financial liberalization in developing countries. See Williamson and Mahar (1998) on the lessons of financial liberalization.

17. Rubin (1998) also suggests that the IFIs should consider conditioning access to loans on countries' willingness to improve their transparency. In addition, he notes that authorities in the major countries could consider making access to their markets by foreign banks conditional on a strong home-country supervisory regime (as demonstrated by adherence to the Core Principles). On the latter point, I suspect that the actual leverage associated with such bilateral actions will be less than it seems; see Goldstein (1997a).

the same supervisory standards as private-sector institutions. Even when the government doesn't own banks, it often exerts a large adverse influence on credit decisions. The reason governments channel assistance to ailing industries via the banking system rather than on the government budget is that the former is less visible to the public.[18] Minimum transparency guidelines would take away much of that incentive.[19] As the Asian financial crisis has demonstrated, if nothing is done to alter the incentives for excessive government ownership and involvement in the banking system, an important source of large credit losses is likely to escape proper supervision.

A second useful revision to the Core Principles would be to alter the capital adequacy guideline for banks. The Core Principles urge countries with volatile operating environments to consider imposing higher capital requirements than the 8 percent risk-weighted minimum. But experience has shown that this advice has seldom been taken. Taken as a group, emerging-market economies have not yet set national capital requirements much above the Basle minimum, nor do their banks typically actually hold capital much above those in countries with much more stable operating environments.[20] The present approach gives the same risk weight to a commercial loan in say, Venezuela as it does to one, say, in the United States (despite the greater risk associated with the former). The *preferred approach should be to treat regulatory capital for credit risk much closer to the way regulatory capital is treated for market risk, that is, closer to a portfolio, "value at risk" approach*; this should produce more sensible capital requirements for countries facing higher risk.[21]

Yet a third helpful amendment to the Core Principles would be to *add the elements of an efficient national bankruptcy law to the list.* Too often, developing economies do not have such laws at all, or, where they do have them, they often make it very difficult and time-consuming for creditors to recover the collateral behind delinquent loans, thereby rendering more disorderly efforts to reschedule private debt and adding to

---

18. A dramatic example of this process at work has been China's use of the state-owned banks to fund loss-making state-owned enterprises. See Lardy (1998) for a discussion.

19. In Goldstein (1997a), I recommend, inter alia, that the government budget include all government costs and quasi-fiscal operations that involve the banking system; that data be published annually on nonperforming loans in state-owned banks (on a basis that permits comparison with privately owned banks); that the nature and extent of government instructions to banks on the allocation of credit be disclosed publicly; and that state-owned banks be subject to an external audit by a private independent external auditor and that the results of that audit be published.

20. See Goldstein (1997a).

21. See Institute of International Finance (1998) for a discussion of many of the issues associated with moving away from the current Basle risk weights toward a portfolio approach to credit risk.

banks' credit losses.[22] Sachs (1995) has made a strong case for why an international bankruptcy code that incorporated certain essential principles and mechanisms found in the domestic context (i.e., an automatic stay to prevent a creditor grab race, provision of working capital to the restructured entity, and preclusion of holdouts and free riding by majority voting and/or cramdown by a bankruptcy court) would be of great benefit. It appears, however, that the practical obstacles to such an international code are too formidable to overcome.[23] But this does not mean that the minimum elements of a good bankruptcy law could not be implemented at the national level.[24] The Core Principles should set out these minimum elements to guide national policymakers in their reform efforts.

Transparency and Disclosure in International Financial Markets

Improving transparency and disclosure in international financial markets took on higher priority after the Mexican peso crisis (with the establishment of the IMF's SDDS), and it should remain as one of the key agenda items in any Halifax II discussions. Further progress would be particularly welcome on three fronts.

To begin with, all parties would profit from the availability of more comprehensive, more frequent, and more timely data on the *maturity and currency composition of external debt*, including the debt owed by banks and corporations in emerging economies. The BIS (1998) already publishes data on the maturity, sectoral, and nationality distribution of international bank lending to selected emerging economies; one of those series is published semiannually and one quarterly.[25] Indeed, any analyst who was paying attention to that data in the four to five year run-up to the crisis would have found useful hints on the build-up of the liquidity/currency mismatches highlighted in chapter 2.[26] Many market participants were apparently either not aware of these data or did not accord them much weight in their risk analysis. Other useful data on external debt are published by the World Bank and the Organization for Economic Cooperation

---

22. See Eichengreen and Portes (1995) and Goldstein and Turner (1996).

23. See Eichengreen and Portes (1995, 1998) and Calvo and Goldstein (1996).

24. Litan (1998) argues that once a common approach is applied to crisis situations on a national level, important international precedents will have been set. He argues that crisis countries should pass simple bankruptcy legislation (if none exists).

25. The semiannual series on international bank lending is prepared on a globally consolidated basis, whereas the quarterly series is not.

26. See, for example, the data on international bank lending to South Korea discussed in Ito (1998a).

and Development (OECD), and the IMF's SDDS sets out some requirements for the publication of central government debt and for the external position of the banking system.

Given the important role that liquidity and currency mismatches in the banking and corporate sector played in the Asian financial crisis, it would be useful to try to improve the information publicly available on short-term private debt. Specifically, it would be worth investigating whether the *BIS banking data could be published with a shorter time lag* (the lag is presently on the order of four to six months), if the *maturity distribution at the short end (one year or less) could be disaggregated further* (say, to include breakdowns for one month, three months, six months, and one year), *if the globally consolidated series on international bank lending could be made available quarterly*, and if better information on the *currency distribution (for the major currencies) of short-term debt could be made available.*[27] Likewise, the Indonesian crisis highlights the desirability of having more comprehensive information available on the size and composition of the nonfinancial corporate sector's external position. As these data on the maturity and currency composition of external private-sector debt are upgraded, several of the key series should be included in the IMF's SDDS.

Market discipline would similarly be aided if better data were publicly available on *net international reserves,* that is, on gross international reserves less reserve-related liabilities (including commitments in the forward exchange market). At present, the IMF's SDDS "requires" monthly data on gross official reserves but only "encourages" the publication of reserve-related liabilities (as relevant). In view of the difficulties of gauging net reserves in both the Thai and South Korean financial crises, it would be desirable to amend the SDDS so as to make both reserve-related liabilities and forward exchange commitments *required* variables.

Yet a third desirable transparency/disclosure initiative would be to attempt to move closer to an *international harmonized definition of nonperforming bank loans (prepared in accordance with international accounting standards) and to publish such data on at least a semiannual basis as a required element of the SDDS.*[28] As noted in chapter 2 (table 5), official estimates of nonperforming bank loans grossly underestimated the true extent of the problem in many of the Asian-crisis countries, and this experience has

---

27. The World Bank publishes comprehensive data on the currency denomination of long-term foreign debt, but identifying the currency composition of all short-term debt is more problematic.

28. See IMF (1997a), Goldstein (1997a), and the Basle Committee on Banking Supervision (1997) for a discussion of what elements would need to be considered in framing such a harmonized definition. The impact of changes in the definition should not be underestimated. For example, it has been estimated that when Mexico moved to a definition of nonperforming loans based on international accounting standards, that change itself led to a near doubling of nonperforming loans in the banking system; see IMF (1997a).

been repeated over and over in the run-up to previous banking crises.[29] The sooner we can get to a situation where market participants can make a better-informed decision about the health of the banking system, the sooner are we likely to get risk premiums that bear a closer relationship to the true risks at hand.[30]

IMF Surveillance

After every major financial crisis, there is a call for making *IMF surveillance more effective*. The Asian crisis is no exception. There were apparently two problems. In those cases where the IMF early on saw crisis vulnerability building and recommended corrective actions (external-sector problems in Thailand and banking problems in South Korea), the IMF's advice was not adopted. And in some other cases, the IMF, much like almost all other analysts, did not see the crisis coming (Indonesia, Malaysia, etc.). At its April 1998 meeting, the IMF's Interim Committee (1998c, 2–3) urged the IMF, inter alia, "to intensify its surveillance of financial sector issues and capital flows . . . and to develop a 'tiered response,' whereby countries that are believed to be seriously off course in their policies are given increasingly strong warnings."

A few years ago, I undertook a wide-ranging analysis of IMF surveillance (Goldstein 1995). From the perspective of the Asian crisis, several points merit emphasis.

While an intensification of surveillance on financial-sector issues and capital flows may help some in identifying crises at an earlier stage, it does not deal with the issue of how to get countries to take the IMF's diagnosis and policy prescriptions more seriously. Recent efforts to make peer pressure more effective—including regional initiatives like the one laid out in the Manila Framework—are worthy of support, but there are likely to be limits to how far such pressure exerted behind closed doors can go in encouraging errant borrowers to take early corrective actions. In the end, the IMF membership needs to accept the reality that for countries that have access to international capital markets, the most potent channel for giving IMF surveillance more punch is by affecting the market's evaluation of a country's policies. In other words, *the IMF needs to affect the information set of those private market participants who move large amounts of funds across national borders*. It is not enough to simply pass information about crisis vulnerabilities within the official sector.

---

29. See Goldstein and Turner (1996).

30. Goldstein and Turner (1996) provide two examples of the types of published information on banking systems that it would be useful to have—for the banking system as a whole and for individual banks.

Since 1994, the IMF has been making public (so long as the country approves) that part of its Article IV country reports that contain the factual information on recent economic developments. Since May 1997, it has also been making available (again, subject to the individual country's approval) summaries of the IMF Executive Board discussion of the Article IV consultation (so-called "Press Information Notices"). But what the IMF does *not* now publish and what would be the most useful to market participants is the IMF staff's evaluation of the country's policies and prospects (that is, the staff appraisal part of the Article IV consultation report). Instead of inching forward every few years by publishing everything but the beef, it's high time for the IMF membership to at least allow those members who are so inclined to publish these Article IV reports. Once a group of the larger economies does this, the process of "competitive transparency" will put strong pressure on the rest to go along.

It is sometimes argued that it is not necessary for the IMF to publish its view of country policies because we have private rating agencies whose raison d'être is to evaluate risk. But there is accumulating evidence (Goldstein and Reinhart forthcoming 1998; Larrain, Reisen, and von Maltzan 1997) that these private credit ratings have done a poor job in anticipating currency and banking crises in emerging economies over the past 25 years, and their performance during the Asian financial crisis certainly has done little to alter that pessimistic finding. In other words, it does appear as if there is room for IMF appraisals to "add value" on crisis vulnerability to what warnings already exist in the market from the major private credit-rating firms. Increasing the availability of economic and financial data will pay dividends, but getting better analysis into the marketplace is also worthy of attention.

Objections to having the IMF share its view more widely with private markets are typically voiced on two counts. One objection is that such disclosure will destroy the frankness and confidentiality of Article IV consultations. But assessments of country policies (at least for the major industrial countries and for some larger emerging economies) have been included in the biannual *World Economic Outlook* for over 15 years, and the consultation process is apparently none the worse for it. Also, it is not necessary to provide the markets with a video cassette that includes every piece of information and every conversation that took place during the consultation in order to transmit the IMF's view of vulnerabilities.

The second objection is more serious. It is that by publishing the appraisals in staff reports, the IMF will be accused of precipitating crises and that this would be inconsistent with its purpose of "giving confidence to members." Two cases might be distinguished. The former is one in which the IMF has the correct diagnosis, and release of its appraisal leads to some market reaction. In this situation, it can be argued that once a country's policies go significantly off track, some correction is inevitable and that it is better to have a smaller market correction early than a full-blown crisis later on. The second case is where the IMF's analysis is faulty, and it leads to a market reaction that (in retrospect) could have been avoided. Given that the ability to recognize crises beforehand is surely going to be subject to some margin of error, this latter situation cannot be ruled out entirely. This is a cost of issuing early warnings that has to be weighed against the benefits to be derived from catching other (presumably more) crises earlier on. Knowing that its diagnosis was going to be public would also, I think, lead over time to an improvement in the quality of these IMF Article IV reports. In addition, I believe the growing empirical literature on early warning indicators of currency and banking crises in emerging economies would help to improve the identification of crisis vulnerabilities.[31] And if the IMF's analysis turned out to be no better, or worse, than that of private-sector groups, then these reports would lose their market impact and the IMF's responsibilities in this area would no doubt be curtailed by its membership.[32]

The truth is that some risk will need to be taken in connection with making IMF surveillance more public if one wants to obtain a significant improvement in its impact. Alternatively, if the official view is that even one false crisis warning is too high a price to pay, then IMF surveillance will continue to be confidential but also of limited effectiveness.

Suppose a decision is made to share more of the IMF's early warnings with the private sector. In addition to the publication of Article IV reports, how should the IMF's message be communicated and to whom? One flawed proposal—which sometimes goes under the heading of "early involvement of the private sector"—would be to communicate that warning confidentially to a group representing large private creditors. The problem here is one of *inside information*. Why should large wholesale investors get this advance warning before small retail investors get it, or why should foreign investors get it before domestic investors? It is one thing to have a standing steering committee of private creditors to facilitate the rescheduling of private debt. In that context, these representative have a legitimate right to be a direct party to these negotiations because it is their claims that are being rescheduled. In addition, the practicalities of negotiating directly with an enormous number of creditors makes a steer-

---

31. See Kaminsky and Reinhart (1996), Goldstein and Reinhart (forthcoming 1998), Frankel and Rose (1996), Eichengreen, Rose, and Wyplosz (1996), and IMF (1998b).

32. Rubin (1998) adopts a middle-ground view of IMF warnings. On the one side, he seems to support the IMF publicizing its concerns about important gaps in countries' disclosure, as well as more frequent and regular publication of a number of IMF documents and analyses, including analyses of countries' financial regulatory and supervisory systems. On the other side, he opposes giving the IMF the responsibility to publicly predict formal warnings of crises (in part because, in his view, it is not possible to reliably predict combustion into crises).

ing committee a sensible representative mechanism. But there is no analogous constraint on sharing information with all investors (more and more IMF reports are being made available on the internet), and large wholesale foreign investors have no special claim to early information from the IMF.

As regards the vehicles that should be used to carry the IMF's early warnings, I can see benefit in incorporating these warnings in the *World Economic Outlook*, in the annual *International Capital Markets Report*, and in speeches of the IMF management. Because the timing of those reports and speeches (cum the issue of Article IV reports) is spread throughout the year, they ought to provide enough flexibility to capture variations over time in the IMF's concerns about individual countries. The advantage of incorporating warnings in these reports relative to direct bulletins on individual countries is that one can more easily place country prospects within a broader setting and can vary the language across countries and over time to convey a "tiered response" to perceived vulnerabilities. Also, the direct bulletin approach suffers from the disadvantage that absence of a warning may be read by the market as signifying "no problem." As with reports of central banks, the market should over time be able to "read between the lines" to figure out when the IMF is unusually concerned about an individual country's situation.

To sum up, notwithstanding the mantra on the importance of strengthening IMF surveillance in Interim Committee communiqués, the IMF's member countries have for a long time been ambivalent about whether they really want the IMF to engage in "firm surveillance." This reflects the fact that the membership wants the IMF to be *both* a trusted inside advisor to countries and a whistle blower for financial crises. Where the whistle-blowing role conflicts with the inside-advisor role, they usually have opted for the latter. In my view, the Asian financial crisis is but the latest evidence that the membership should change course and begin to "tilt" toward giving pride of place to the IMF's surveillance responsibility.

Risk Management in Global Financial Institutions

Last but not least, *shoring up risk management in global financial institutions* deserves to be part of the Halifax II agenda. As hinted at in chapter 2, a troubling aspect of the Asian financial crisis is that banks in major creditor countries apparently exercised rather poor credit evaluation and risk management in their lending decisions. Coming on top of earlier well publicized failures at Barings, Daiwa, Morgan Grenfell, Sumitomo, and Hokkaido Takusheku, the Asian crisis has driven home the message that improvements in the international financial architecture must encompass the industrial countries as well developing ones, and lenders as well as borrowers.

A comprehensive review of the prudential and supervisory framework in industrial countries would take us beyond the manageable scope of this book. As an illustration of what needs to be done, however, let me draw attention to a recent Group of Thirty (1997) effort aimed at promoting better understanding and management of risk at large internationally active commercial banks (the major participants in large-value payment systems) and at the largest investment banks. Because a growing volume of international financial transactions is heavily concentrated in this group of "core institutions," it is essential that these institutions get risk management right.[33]

After surveying and studying the risk management practices of these global players, the Group of Thirty's (1997) study group came up with a set of recommendations for the financial-services industry, global auditors, financial supervisors, and industrial-country legislatures. Among that set, the following deserve particular mention and support in connection with the Halifax II discussions (Group of Thirty 1997, 27–8).

- Acting as a group, *core institutions* should: (1) voluntarily create "a standing committee to promulgate and review global principles for managing risk, covering the full range of management control functions; the full range of risks in a global firm; the efficacy of risk-reduction strategies; and the type, format, and location of information to be maintained by all institutions; (2) subject their worldwide operations to expanded review by a single, independent, external audit firm or firm group, and agree upon more consistent and meaningful disclosure of financial and risk information on a globally consolidated basis; and (3) support efforts to agree upon high quality, uniform accounting standards internationally."

- *Global auditors* should: "work with global firms, audit standard bodies and supervisors to achieve an agreed upon approach to financial statement audits and other information for portraying risk."

- *Financial supervisors* should "agree upon a lead coordinator for all global financial institutions; . . . formulate standards for exchanges, clearinghouses and settlement systems, including risk management and financial stability; protection of customer assets, funds and positions; and netting, contract enforceability and insolvency."

Until one sees the actual global risk management principles produced by the industry standard committee, it is impossible to know whether

---

33. For example, the Group of Thirty report (1997) notes that just 20 banks clear and settle 70 percent of the dollar leg of the foreign-exchange transactions going through CHIPS. And with the recent wave of mergers and acquisitions in the financial industry—particularly in the United States—concentration in the industry is on the rise.

this Group of Thirty initiative will live up to its promise. But from the standpoint of dealing with potential weak links in the chain of systemic risk, it goes in the right direction.

The *set of Halifax II reforms proposed* in this chapter *should become part of the action agenda for the next four or five G-8 economic summits (beginning with the Birmingham summit in May 1998) and for the IMF's Interim Committee.* The aim should be to forge a broad consensus on the need for such measures, set explicit target dates for their implementation, and request a series of progress reports that monitor how far countries have come in meeting their commitments.

5

Lessons of the Asian Crisis and Concluding Remarks

No study of financial crises would be complete without some mention of the lessons learned. Because the Asian financial crises has so many interrelated origins and because the geographical scope of the crisis has been so wide, it generates a longer set of potential candidates than most other crises. My nominations for the *top 10 list of lessons learned* from, or reinforced by, the Asian crisis would be the following:

1. Leaving reform of the financial sector and of the prudential/supervisory framework to late in the economic development process is a bad idea—even when the country's macroeconomic-policy record and growth performance place it in the first division of emerging economies. When the financial markets finally discover the true (sorry) state of balance sheets in the financial sector, the cost (in terms of both reduced growth and the fiscal costs of recapitalizing the banking system) can be enormous.

2. The composition of foreign borrowing deserves as much attention as the overall debt burden. In particular, a high and rapidly rising ratio of short-term debt to net international reserves has (ever since the Mexican peso crisis) become a red flag for financial market operators— especially when reserves have been plummeting in the course of defending an overvalued fixed exchange rate. The original saving obtained from shortening the maturity and denominating external debt in foreign currency is likely to be swamped by the ultimate price paid if rollover and currency risk ignite a successful speculative attack.

3. Rapid expansion of bank and nonbank credit (far in excess of the growth of the real economy), cum high concentration of credit to the real estate and equity markets, is almost always a harbinger of trouble, in developing and industrial countries alike. The risk is multiplied when lenders don't do careful analysis of creditworthiness (taking property as collateral instead) and when high loan-to-valuation ratios and low bank capital don't provide much of a cushion when the credit cycle turns south.

4. Large current-account deficits that are used to finance investment may render economies less vulnerable to speculative attacks than those used almost exclusively to finance a boom in consumption, but if the quality of that investment is poor, the former can come to the same unhappy end as the latter.

5. Efforts to promote financial and capital account liberalization without first strengthening the prudential framework—such as the ill-fated Bangkok International Banking Facility in Thailand—are a recipe for disaster.

6. Long-standing weaknesses in the economy that lenders seemingly ignored for long periods of time can take on a different character in the midst of crises elsewhere in the region. Once the process of contagion begins, it takes bold and determined defensive and reform measures to stem the tide in individual countries—especially if a lack of transparency and disclosure make it difficult for investors to differentiate weak from strong firms.

7. Overshooting of exchange rates and equity prices can be much larger than we thought in an atmosphere of political instability, uncertainty about reform, and wide-ranging contagion.

8. It's much tougher to battle your way out of a crisis when the region's largest economy is struggling with its own macroeconomic, financial, and exchange rate problems (Japan) than when (as in Mexico's case) that regional hub (the United States) is in good overall shape.

9. The distinction that was drawn after the Mexican peso crisis between sovereign debt and private debt (in the G-10 report [1996]) has turned out to be not nearly so neat and tidy. When much of the banking system becomes insolvent, debt that starts out in the private sector doesn't stay there long. If we want spreads on emerging-market paper to reflect true underlying risks and if we want market discipline to operate tolerably well, something needs to be done to reduce the moral hazard associated with providing guarantees and other forms of financial support to large uninsured private creditors—both within the country and from abroad. Unless these creditors are made to absorb an equitable part of the adjustment burden, the political sup-

port for IMF-led rescue packages will be very difficult to sustain. Relying more and at an earlier stage on (ad hoc) debt rescheduling to handle private-sector insolvencies is the only way to get these rescue packages back to a reasonable size. Forsaking early intervention to bail out private creditors may make management in the current crisis subject to higher short-term volatility, but this is intrinsic to reducing the frequency of serious crises in the future.

10. There's nothing like a major crisis to focus people's minds on why it is important to improve the international financial architecture. In this sense, there is no better time to put forth a specific agenda for improving the international financial architecture. The emphasis should be on reducing moral hazard and increasing the orderliness and flexibility in private debt rescheduling, convincing developing countries to implement strong international prudential standards, improving transparency and disclosure in international financial markets, putting more punch in IMF surveillance, and shoring up risk management in global financial firms.

The Asian financial crisis has also raised a lot of questions about the future role of the IMF. Despite the depth and breadth of the Asian financial crisis and the limited success achieved so far in combating it, the successful resolution of this crisis does not require a new IMF. Much more has been right than wrong about the overall design of these official rescue packages, and there are mechanisms that if utilized more fully in the future can improve the market discipline and burden-sharing aspects. Those who argue for abolishing the IMF have forgotten the lessons of the 1920s and 1930s, and those who maintain that the crisis would already be over if the IMF simply supplied the crisis countries with large liquidity injections (cum little macroeconomic or structural policy conditionality) are engaged in wishful thinking. Denying the IMF the financial resources it needs to do its job will be harmful to the economic and foreign-policy interests of the United States.

A sustained turn in the Asian financial crisis will come when the crisis countries have made enough progress in implementing structural reforms (especially in their financial sectors) to convince markets that the factors that gave rise to the crisis have really changed, and when there has been enough rescheduling of private debt to reduce uncertainty and to make creditors comfortable enough to provide new lending.

Appendix
List of Core Principles for Effective
Banking Supervision

Preconditions for Effective Banking Supervision

1. An effective system of banking supervision will have clear responsibilities and objectives for each agency involved in the supervision of banking organizations. Each such agency should possess operational independence and adequate resources. A suitable legal framework for banking supervision is also necessary, including provisions relating to authorization of banking organizations and their ongoing supervision; powers to address compliance with laws as well as safety and soundness concerns; and legal protection for supervisors. Arrangements for sharing information between supervisors and protecting the confidentiality of such information should be in place.

Licensing and Structure

2. The permissible activities of institutions that are licensed and subject to supervision as banks must be clearly defined, and the use of the work "bank" in names should be controlled as far as possible.

3. The licensing authority must have the right to set criteria and reject applications for establishments that do not meet the standards set. The licensing process, at a minimum, should consist of an assessment of the banking organization's ownership structure, directors and senior management, its operating plan and internal controls, and its projected financial condition, including its capital base; where the proposed owner or parent organization is a foreign bank, the prior consent of its home country supervisor should be obtained.

4. Banking supervisors must have the authority to review and reject and proposals to transfer significant ownership or controlling interests in existing banks to other parties.

5. Banking supervisors must have the authority to establish criteria for reviewing major acquisitions or investments by a bank and ensuring that corporate affiliations or structures do not expose the bank to undue risks or hinder effective supervision.

Prudential Regulations and Requirements

6. Banking supervisors must set prudent and appropriate minimum capital adequacy requirements for all banks. Such requirements should reflect the risks that the banks undertake, and must define the components of capital, bearing in mind their ability to absorb losses. At least for internationally active banks, these requirements must not be less than those established in the Basle Capital Adequacy Accord and its amendments.

7. An essential past of any supervisory system is the evaluation of a bank's policies, practices and procedures related to the granting of loans and making of investments and the ongoing management of the loan and investment portfolios.

8. Banking supervisors must be satisfied that banks establish and adhere to adequate policies, practices and procedures for evaluating the quality of assets and the adequacy of loan loss provisions and loan loss reserves.

9. Banking supervisors must be satisfied that banks have management information systems that enable management to identify concentrations within the portfolio and supervisors must set prudential limits to restrict bank exposures to single borrowers or groups of related borrowers.

10. In order to prevent abuses arising from connected lending, banking supervisors must have in place requirements that banks lend to related companies and individuals on an arm's-length basis, that such extensions of credit are effectively monitored, and that other appropriate steps are taken to control or mitigate the risks.

11. Banking supervisors must be satisfied that banks have adequate policies and procedures for identifying, monitoring, and controlling country risk and transfer risk in their international lending and investment activities, and for maintaining appropriate reserves against such risks.

12. Banking supervisors must be satisfied that banks have in place systems that accurately measure, monitor and adequately control market risks;

supervisors should have powers to impose specific limits and/or a specific capital charge on market risk exposures, if warranted.

13. Banking supervisors must be satisfied that banks have in place a comprehensive risk management process (including appropriate board and senior management oversight) to identify, measure, monitor and control all other material risks and, where appropriate, to hold capital against these risks.

14. Banking supervisors must determine that banks have in place internal controls that are adequate for the nature and scale of their business. These should include clear arrangements for delegating authority and responsibility; separation of the functions that involve committing the bank, paying away its funds, and accounting for its assets and liabilities; reconciliation of these processes; safeguarding its assets; and appropriate independent internal or external audit and compliance functions to test adherence to these controls as well as applicable laws and regulations.

15. Banking supervisors must determine that banks have adequate policies, practices, and procedures in place, including strict "know-your-customer" rules, that promote high ethical and professional standards in the financial sector and prevent the bank being used, intentionally or unintentionally, by criminal elements.

Methods of Ongoing Banking Supervision

16. An effective banking supervisory system should consist of some form of both on-site and off-site supervision.

17. Banking supervisors must have regular contact with bank management and thorough understanding of the institution's operations.

18. Banking supervisors must have a means of collecting, reviewing and analyzing prudential reports and statistical returns from banks on a solo and consolidated basis.

19. Banking supervisors must have a means of independent validation of supervisory information either through on-site examinations or use of external auditors.

20. As essential element of banking supervision is the ability of the supervisors to supervise the banking group on a consolidated basis.

Information Requirements

21. Banking supervisors must be satisfied that each bank maintains adequate records drawn up in accordance with consistent accounting policies and practices that enable the supervisor to obtain a true and fair view of the financial condition of the bank and the profitability

of its business, and that the bank publishes on a regular basis financial statements that fairly reflect its condition.

Formal Powers of Supervisors

22. Banking supervisors must have at their disposal adequate supervisory measures to bring about timely corrective action when banks fail to meet prudential requirements (such as minimum capital adequacy ratios), when there are regulatory violations, or where depositors are threatened in any other way. In extreme circumstances, this should include the ability to revoke the banking license or recommend its revocation.

Cross-border Banking

23. Banking supervisors must practice global consolidated supervision over their internationally-active banking organizations, adequately monitoring and applying appropriate prudential norms to all aspects of the business conducted by these banking organizations worldwide, primarily at their foreign branches, joint ventures and subsidiaries.

24. A key component of consolidated supervision is establishing contact and information exchange with the various other supervisors involved, primarily host country supervisory authorities.

25. Banking supervisors must require the local operations of foreign banks to be conducted to the same high standards as are required of domestic institutions and must have powers to share information needed by the home country supervisors of those banks for the purpose of carrying out consolidated supervision.

References

Armey, Richard. 1998. IMF Must Stop Subsidizing Irresponsible Risk-Taking, Armey Declares. Press Release, Office of the House Majority Leader. Washington: US House of Representatives (5 March).

Bank for International Settlements (BIS). 1997. *67th Annual Report*. Basle: Bank for International Settlements.

Bank for International Settlements. 1998. *The Maturity, Sectoral, and Nationality Distribution of International Bank Lending*. Basle: Bank for International Settlements.

Basle Committee on Banking Supervision. 1997. *Core Principles for Effective Banking Supervision*. Basle: Basle Committee on Banking Supervision.

Benston, George, and George Kaufman. 1988. *Risk and Solvency Regulation of Depository Institutions: Past Policies and Current Options*. Monograph Series in Finance and Economics. New York: New York University Press.

Benston, George, and George Kaufman. 1997. FDICIA after Five Years. *Journal of Economic Perspectives* 11, no. 3: 139–58.

Bergsten, C. Fred. 1996. The Case for APEC. *The Economist* (6 January).

Bergsten, C. Fred. 1997. The Asian Monetary Crisis: Proposed Remedies. Testimony before the Committee on Banking and Financial Services. Washington: US House of Representatives (13 November).

Bergsten, C. Fred. 1998. The Trade Implications of the Asian Financial Crisis. Testimony before the Committee on Finance. Washington: US Senate (4 February).

Bhattacharya, Amar, Stijn Claessens, and Leonardo Hernandez. 1997. Recent Financial Market Turbulence in Southeast Asia. Washington: World Bank (October). Photocopy.

Calomiris, Charles. 1997. *The Postmodern Bank Safety Net: Lessons from Developed and Developing Economies*. Washington: American Enterprise Institute.

Calomiris, Charles. 1998. Statement before the Joint Economic Committee of the US Congress. Washington (24 February).

Calvo, Guillermo, and Morris Goldstein. 1996. Crisis Prevention and Crisis Management after Mexico: What Role for the Official Sector? In *Private Capital Flows to Emerging Markets After the Mexican Crisis*, ed. by Guillermo Calvo, Morris Goldstein, and Eduard Hochreiter. Washington: Institute for International Economics.

Calvo, Sara, and Carmen Reinhart. 1996. Capital Flows to Latin America: Is There Evidence of Contagion? In *Private Capital Flows to Emerging Economies After the Mexican Crisis*, ed. by Guillermo Calvo, Morris Goldstein, and Eduardo Hochreiter. Washington: Institute for International Economics.

Caprio, Gerard, and Daniela Klingebiel. 1996. Bank Insolvencies: Cross-Country Experience. Washington: World Bank. Photocopy.

Chote, Robert. 1998. Financial Crises: The Lessons of Asia. In *Financial Crises in Asia*. London: Centre for Economic Policy Research.

Claessens, Stijn. 1998. Financial Sector Weaknesses. Paper presented at the World Bank and University of Maryland Seminar on Capital Flow Volatility and Early Warning of Financial Crises in College Park, Maryland (March).

Claessens, Stijn, and Thomas Glaessner. 1997. *Are Financial Sector Weaknesses Undermining the Asian Miracle?* Washington: World Bank.

Cline, William. 1995. *International Debt Reexamined*. Washington: Institute for International Economics.

Cline, William, and Kevin Barnes. 1997. *Spreads and Risk in Emerging Market Lending*. IIF Research Paper No. 97-1. Washington: Institute for International Finance (November). Photocopy.

Corden, Max, and Michael Dooley. 1989. Issues in Debt Strategy: An Overview. In *Analytical Issues in Debt*, ed. by Jacob Frenkel, Michael Dooley, and Peter Wickham. Washington: International Monetary Fund.

Dodsworth, J., and D. Mihaljek. 1997. *Hong Kong, China: Growth, Structural Change and Economic Stability During the Transition*. IMF Occasional Paper No. 152. Washington: International Monetary Fund.

Dooley, Michael. 1997. *A Model of Crises in Emerging Markets*. NBER Working Paper No. 6300. Cambridge, MA: National Bureau of Economic Research (December).

Dziobek, Claudia, and Ceyla Pazarbasioglu. 1997. *Lessons from Systemic Bank Restructuring: A Survey of 24 Countries*. IMF Working Paper No. 97/161. Washington: International Monetary Fund (December).

Eichengreen, Barry, and Richard Portes. 1995. *Crisis, What Crisis? Orderly Workouts for Sovereign Debtors*. London: Centre for Economic Policy Research.

Eichengreen, Barry, and Richard Portes. 1996. Managing the Next Mexico. In *From Halifax to Lyons: What Has Been Done About Crisis Management?* ed. by Peter B. Kenen. Essays in International Finance No. 200. Princeton: International Finance Section, Princeton University (October).

Eichengreen, Barry, and Richard Portes. 1998. A New Approach to Managing Financial Crises. In *Financial Crises in Asia*, ed. by Robert Chote. London: Centre for Economic Policy Research.

Eichengreen, Barry, Andrew Rose, and Charles Wyplosz. 1996. *Contagious Currency Crises*. NBER Working Paper No. 5681. Cambridge, MA: National Bureau of Economic Research (July).

Eschweiler, Bernhard. 1997a. Emerging Asia: The Fallout after the FX Crisis. *Asian Financial Markets*. Singapore: JP Morgan (17 October).

Eschweiler, Bernhard. 1997b. Did the Market See the Asian Crisis Coming? Paper presented at the World Bank Conference on The Asian Crisis, Washington (4 October).

Eschweiler, Bernhard. 1998. *Asian Financial Markets*. Singapore: JP Morgan (16 January).

Farrow, Maureen A. 1997. Asia Unravels. Investment Research. Toronto: Loewen, Ondaatje, McCutcheon Limited (27 November).

Feldman, Ron, and Arthur Rolnick. 1998. Fixing FDICIA: A Plan to Address the Too-Big-To-Fail Problem. *Federal Reserve Bank of Minneapolis Annual Report* 12, no. 1 (Special Issue) (March).

Feldstein, Martin. 1998. Refocusing the IMF. *Foreign Affairs* (February).

Fernald, John, Hali Edison, and Prakash Loungani. 1998. Was China the First Domino? Assessing Links Between China and the Rest of Emerging Asia. Washington: Board of Governors of the Federal Reserve System (March). Photocopy.

Fernandez, Roque. 1996. Capital Flows and the Liquidity Shock. In *Private Capital Flows to Emerging Markets After the Mexican Crisis*, ed. by Guillermo Calvo, Morris Goldstein, and Eduard Hochreiter. Washington: Institute for International Economics.

Fischer, Stanley. 1997. *Capital Account Liberalization and the Role of the IMF*. Washington: International Monetary Fund.

Folkerts-Landau, David, Garry Schinasi, Marcel Cassard, Victor Ng, Carmen Reinhart, and Michael Spencer. 1995. Effect of Capital Flows on the Domestic Financial Sectors in APEC Developing Countries. In *Capital Flows in the APEC Region*, ed. by Mohsin Khan and Carmen Reinhart. IMF Occasional Paper No. 122. Washington: International Monetary Fund (March).

Frankel, Jeffrey, and Andrew Rose. 1996. Currency Crashes in Emerging Markets. *Journal of International Economics* 41, no. 3/4: 351–66.

Garcia, Gillian. 1998. Deposit Insurance. In *Preventing Banking Crises*, ed. by Gerard Caprio, Danny Leipziger, and George Kaufman. Chicago: Federal Reserve Bank of Chicago; Washington: World Bank. Forthcoming.

Garcia, Gillian, and Carl-Johan Lindgren. 1996. *Deposit Insurance and Crisis Management*. Operational Paper No. 96/3. Washington: International Monetary Fund.

Goldstein, Morris. 1995. *The Exchange Rate System and the IMF: A Modest Agenda*. POLICY ANALYSES IN INTERNATIONAL ECONOMICS NO. 39. Washington: Institute for International Economics.

Goldstein, Morris. 1996. Avoiding Future Mexicos. In *From Halifax to Lyons: What Has Been Done about Crisis Management?* ed. by Peter B. Kenen. Essays in International Finance No. 200. Princeton: International Finance Section, Princeton University (October).

Goldstein, Morris. 1997a. *The Case for an International Banking Standard*. POLICY ANALYSES IN INTERNATIONAL ECONOMICS NO. 47. Washington: Institute for International Economics.

Goldstein, Morris. 1997b. Towards an International Banking Standard. *Financial Regulator* 2, no. 2 (September): 11–14.

Goldstein, Morris. 1998a. Commentary: The Causes and Propagation of Financial Stability: Lessons for Policy Makers. In *Maintaining Financial Stability in a Global Economy*, by the Federal Reserve Bank of Kansas City. Kansas City: Federal Reserve Bank of Kansas City.

Goldstein, Morris. 1998b. Banking Crises: International Experience. In *Preventing Banking Crises*, ed. by Gerard Caprio, George Kaufman, and Danny Leipziger. Chicago: Federal Reserve Bank of Chicago; Washington: World Bank. Forthcoming.

Goldstein, Morris, and John Hawkins. 1998. *The Origins of the Asian Financial Turmoil*. Reserve Bank of Australia Research Discussion Paper 980. Sydney: Reserve Bank of Australia (May).

Goldstein, Morris, and Carmen Reinhart. 1998. *Forecasting Financial Crises: Early Warning Signals for Emerging Markets*. POLICY ANALYSES IN INTERNATIONAL ECONOMICS. Washington: Institute for International Economics. Forthcoming.

Goldstein, Morris, and Philip Turner. 1996. *Banking Crises in Emerging Economies: Origins and Policy Options*. BIS Economic Papers No. 46. Basle: Bank for International Settlements.

Grenville, Stephen. 1998. Exchange Rates and Crises. *Contemporary Economic Policy*. Forthcoming.

Group of Ten (G-10). 1996. *The Resolution of Sovereign Liquidity Crises: A Report to the Ministers and Governors*. Basle: Bank for International Settlements; Washington: International Monetary Fund.

Group of Thirty (G-30). 1997. *Global Institutions, National Supervision, and Systemic Risk*. A Study Group Report. Washington: Group of Thirty.

Hale, David. 1997. The East Asian Financial Crisis and the World Economy. Testimony before the House Banking Committee, Washington (13 November).

Hawkins, John, and M. Yiu. 1995. Real and Effective Exchange Rates. *Hong Kong Monetary Authority* 5: 1–11.

Institute of International Finance (IIF). 1998. Report of the Working Group on Capital Adequacy. Washington: Institute for International Finance (March).

International Monetary Fund (IMF). 1997a. *International Capital Markets Report.* Washington: International Monetary Fund.

International Monetary Fund. 1997b. *World Economic Outlook: Interim Assessment.* Washington: International Monetary Fund.

International Monetary Fund. 1998a. *Toward A Framework for Financial Stability.* Washington: International Monetary Fund.

International Monetary Fund. 1998b. *World Economic Outlook.* Washington: International Monetary Fund.

International Monetary Fund. 1998c. Communiqué of the Interim Committee of the Board of Governors of the International Monetary Fund. Washington: International Monetary Fund (16 April).

International Monetary Fund. 1998d. IMF Approves Supplemental Reserve Facility. *IMF Survey* 27, no. 1 (12 January): 7.

International Monetary Fund. 1998e. IMF Lending in 1997 Soars to Near-Record Level as Asian Countries Make Large Drawings. *IMF Survey* 27, no. 3 (9 February): 34.

Ito, Takatoshi. 1998a. Capital Flows in Asia. Paper presented to the NBER conference on Capital Inflows to Emerging Markets, Cambridge, MA, National Bureau of Economic Research, (February).

Ito, Takatoshi. 1998b. Wanted in Japan: A Supply-Side Keynes? Presentation at Columbia University, New York (31 March).

Ito, Takatoshi. 1998c. Bail-Out, Moral Hazard, and Credibility. Paper presented to the Wharton conference on Asian Twin Financial Crises, Tokyo (10 March).

Jardine Fleming. 1997. Asia's Banking Crisis: Estimating the Cost. *Jardine Fleming Research.* Singapore: Jardine Fleming (6 October).

Jen, S. 1998. Asian Crisis: A Déjà Vu of the U.S. S&L Crisis. Singapore: Morgan Stanley (19 February). Photocopy.

Kaminsky, Graciela, and Carmen Reinhart. 1996. *The Twin Crises: The Causes of Banking and Balance of Payments Problems.* Board of Governors of the Federal Reserve System and the International Monetary Fund, International Finance Discussion Paper No. 544. Washington: Board of Governors of the Federal Reserve System.

Kenen, Peter, ed. 1996. *From Halifax to Lyon: What Has Happened to Crisis Management?* Essays in International Finance No. 200. Princeton: Princeton University (October).

Krugman, Paul. 1998a. What Happened to Asia? Cambridge, MA: Economics Department, MIT (January). Photocopy.

Krugman, Paul. 1998b. Will Asia Bounce Back? Cambridge, MA: Economics Department, MIT (March). Photocopy.

Kwan, C. H. 1997. Causes and Consequences of Asia's Currency Crisis. Tokyo: Nomura Research Institute (October). Photocopy.

Lardy, Nicholas. 1998. *China's Unfinished Economic Revolution.* Washington: Brookings Institution. Forthcoming.

Larrain, Guillermo, Helmut Reisen, and Julia von Maltzan. 1997. *Emerging Market Risk and Sovereign Credit Ratings.* OECD Technical Papers No. 124. Paris: Organization for Economic Cooperation and Development (April).

Lincoln, Edward. 1997. Maybe It's the Teacher's Fault: Asian Nations Adopted the Japan Model; Now They're Paying the Price. *U.S. News and World Report* (15 December).

Lindgren, Carl-Johan, Gillian Garcia, and Mathew Saal. 1996. *Bank Soundness and Macroeconomic Policy.* Washington: International Monetary Fund.

Lipsky, John, Larry Brainard, and Karen Parker. 1997. Emerging Markets after Thailand. *Chase Research* (1 October).

Litan, Robert. 1998. *A Three-Step Remedy for Asia's Financial Flu*. Brookings Policy Brief No. 30. Washington: Brookings Institution (February).

Liu, Li-Gang, Marcus Noland, Sherman Robinson, and Zhi Wang. 1998. *Asian Competitive Devaluations*. Working Paper No. 98-2. Washington: Institute for International Economics (January).

Mann, Catherine. 1998. Lenders of Last Resort: National and International. Washington: Institute for International Economics (January). Photocopy.

Mishkin, Frederick. 1997. Asymmetric Information and Financial Crises: A Developing Country Perspective. *Annual World Bank Conference on Development Economics*. Washington: World Bank.

Montiel, Peter, and Carmen Reinhart. 1997. The Dynamics of Capital Movements to Emerging Economies during the 1990s. Williams College and the University of Maryland, (July). Photocopy.

Mussa, Michael. 1986. Nominal Exchange Rate Regimes and the Behavior of Real Exchange Rates. In *Real Business Cycles, Real Exchange Rates and Actual Policies*, ed. by Karl Brunner and Allan Meltzer. Carnegie-Rochester Conference Series on Public Policy No. 25. Amsterdam: North Holland.

Peregrine. 1997. Peregrine Sees Asia Ex-Japan Bad Debts at $500 Billion. Reported by Bloomberg L. P. (11–12 November).

Perry, Guillermo, and Daniel Lederman. 1998. Financial Vulnerability, Spillover Effects, and Contagion: Lessons from the Asian Crisis for Latin America, Latin American, and Caribbean Region. Washington: World Bank (March). Photocopy.

Posen, Adam. 1998. *How Much Is Enough for Japan?* POLICY ANALYSES IN INTERNATIONAL ECONOMICS. Washington: Institute for International Economics. Forthcoming.

Radelet, Steven, and Jeffrey Sachs. 1998. The Onset of the Asian Financial Crisis. Cambridge, MA: Harvard Institute for International Development (February). Photocopy.

Ramos, Ray (for Goldman Sachs). 1998. Banks: A Critical Ingredient to Recovery for Asia. Presentation to World Bank/Asian Development Bank Seminar, Manila (March).

Rubin, Robert. 1998. Strengthening the Architecture of the International Financial System. Remarks delivered at the Brookings Institution, Washington (14 April). US *Treasury News*.

Sachs, Jeffrey. 1995. Do We Need an International Lender of Last Resort? Frank Graham Memorial Lecture. Princeton: Princeton University (April). Photocopy.

Sachs, Jeffrey. 1997. Power Unto Itself. *Financial Times* (11 December).

Shultz, George, William Simon, and Walter Wriston. 1998. Who Needs the IMF? *Wall Street Journal* (3 February).

Stiglitz, Joseph. 1998. Macroeconomic Dimensions of the East Asian Crisis. In *Financial Crises and Asia*, ed. by Robert Chote. London: Centre for Economic Policy Research.

Summers, Lawrence. 1996. Introduction. In *From Halifax to Lyons: What Has Been Done About Crisis Management?* Essays in International Finance No. 200. Princeton: Princeton University (October).

Thurow, Lester. 1998. Asia: The Collapse and the Cure. *New York Review of Books* (5 February).

Volcker, Paul. 1997. Global Markets and the Emerging Economies. Lecture in Honor of Fritz Leutwiler, University of Zurich, Switzerland (15 December).

Walsh, Max. 1997. *Sydney Morning Herald*. Sydney (October) .

Williamson, John. 1996. The Case for a Common Basket Peg for East Asian Currencies. Paper presented at the international conference on Exchange Rate Policies in Emerging Asian Countries, Seoul, South Korea (15–16 November).

Williamson, John, and Molly Mahar. 1998. A Review of Financial Liberalization. South Asia Region Discussion Paper. Washington: World Bank (January). Photocopy.

World Bank. 1998. *Global Development Finance*, vol. 1. Analysis and Summary Tables. Washington: World Bank.

Young, Soogil, and Jae-Jung Kwon. 1998. The Korean Economy under the IMF Program. Seoul: Korea Institute for International Economic Policy (January). Photocopy.

Other Publications from the
Institute for International Economics

POLICY ANALYSES IN INTERNATIONAL ECONOMICS Series

Trade and Labor Standards
Kimberly Ann Elliott and Richard Freeman
Leading Indicators of Financial Crises in the Emerging Economies
Morris Goldstein and Carmen Reinhart
Prospects for Western Hemisphere Free Trade
Gary Clyde Hufbauer and Jeffrey J. Schott
The Future of US Foreign Aid
Carol Lancaster
The Asian Financial Crisis and Global Adjustment
Li-Gang Liu, Marcus Noland, Sherman Robinson, and Zhi Wang
The Economics of Korean Unification
Marcus Noland
International Lender of Last Resort
Catherine L. Mann
A Primer on US External Balance
Catherine L. Mann
Foreign Direct Investment and Development:
The New Policy Agenda for Developing Countries and Economies in Transition
Theodore Moran
How Much is Enough for Japan?
Adam Posen
Globalization, the NAIRU, and Monetary Policy
Adam Posen
Foreign Enterprises in the Chinese Marketplace
Daniel Rosen
Measuring the Costs of Protection in China
Zhang Shuguang, Zhang Yansheng, and Wan Zhongxin

DISTRIBUTORS OUTSIDE THE UNITED STATES

Canada
RENOUF BOOKSTORE
5369 Canotek Road, Unit 1,
Ottawa, Ontario K1J 9J3, Canada
(tel: (613) 745-2665
fax: (613) 745-7660)

Caribbean
SYSTEMATICS STUDIES LIMITED
St. Augustine Shopping Centre
Eastern Main Road, St. Augustine
Trinidad and Tobago, West Indies
(tel: 868-645-8466; fax: 868-645-8467)

Japan
UNITED PUBLISHERS SERVICES, LTD.
Kenkyu-Sha Bldg.
9, Kanda Surugadai 2-Chome
Chiyoda-Ku, Tokyo 101, Japan
(tel: 81-3-3291-4541; fax: 81-3-3292-8610)
email: saito@ups.co.jp

Visit our website at:
http://www.iie.com

E-mail orders to:
iiecon@pmds.com